Eternal Springs

Geoffrey Duncan is the compiler of numerous anthologies for worship that have sold over 50,000 copies and are used in churches and Christian communities throughout the world.

They include *Shine On, Star of Bethlehem* (co-published with Christian Aid and CAFOD), *Timeless Prayers for Peace* and *A Lifetime of Blessing*.

Other Geoffrey Duncan titles available from the Canterbury Press

Entertaining Angels: An anthology in sharing
Christ's hospitality   1-85311-642-4

   'a clarion call to empathy, prayer and action'

Harvest for the World: A Christian Aid/CAFOD
worship resource on sharing the world's resources   1-85311-574-6

Let Justice Roll Down: A Christian Aid/CAFOD
anthology for Lent, Holy Week and Easter   1-85311-555-X

A Lifetime of Blessing: Prayers and Benedictions
for all the days of your life   1-85311-573-8

Seeing Christ in Others: An anthology for
worship, meditation and mission   1-85311-441-3

   'its diversity makes for originality . . . it is rich in new
   insights' *Methodist Recorder*

Shine On, Star of Bethlehem: A Christian
Aid/CAFOD worship anthology for Advent,
Christmas and Epiphany   1-85311-588-6

   'there is something for everyone here' *Church Times*

Timeless Prayers for Peace   1-85311-515-0

   'an inspirational tool with which to build broken
   community' *Reform*

Wisdom is Calling: An anthology of hope, and
agenda for change   1-85311-243-7

wwww.canterburypress.co.uk

Eternal Springs

An anthology of hope

Compiled by Geoffrey Duncan

CANTERBURY
PRESS
Norwich

© The contributors 2006
© In this compilation Geoffrey Duncan 2006

First published in 2006 by the Canterbury Press Norwich
(a publishing imprint of Hymns Ancient & Modern Limited,
a registered charity)
9–17 St Alban's Place, London N1 0NX

www.scm-canterburypress.co.uk

British Library Cataloguing in Publication data

A catalogue record for this book is available
from the British Library

ISBN 1-85311-718-8/978-1-85311-718-3

Typeset by Regent Typesetting, London
Printed and bound by
William Clowes Ltd, Beccles, Suffolk

Dedication

This anthology of Hope is dedicated to my second granddaughter Maya.

Maya, always remember that your name means light . . . vision.

You are growing up in a world where people need plenty of hope and plenty of light in their lives. Always aim to make your hopes and visions come true so that children, women and men, whoever they are and wherever they live, in our international world, will have opportunities for a good life.

Contents

Introduction

The idea for an anthology of hope came to mind about two years ago. In conversation with a variety of people, I met with the belief that this is what we need at this time – hope for a world in disarray. We have become accustomed to threats of war and terror, erosion of human rights, and governments whose laws expose the vulnerable to iniquity and injustice.

One huge form of injustice is encountered by refugees and asylum seekers. However, there is hope when people like the Revd Sally Thomas stand up, speak out and take action for justice. Her intervention was tremendously important, indeed essential, for the life of an Afghani Christian who must be allowed to remain in the UK. He must not be returned to Afghanistan. Sally and her husband gave him shelter in their home. Sally spoke with me about this young man and asked that he and I should speak at times on the phone. This was a time for listening. When deportation papers were issued he ran away from Manchester to London. He was traced and had to report regularly to a Home Office centre. One day he sensed danger but too late, he was arrested and sent to a detention centre. Fortunately, he was able to maintain contact with the minister. Eventually the day came for him to be deported from Manchester airport. The minister and three church members leafleted the airport with information on why he should not be flown back to Afghanistan. A passenger refused to fly and the pilot refused to fly him back to Afghanistan via Dubai. The minister and three church members were removed from the airport by police. The young Afghani was not deported but placed again in detention. This activity resulted in a review of his case. Many months later he was given status with indefinite leave to stay. He is now happily settled in north London, has employment and pays taxes. If this young Afghani Christian had been deported he may well have been dead by now.

Then there is the unacceptable face of global water privatization, which in coming decades will severely restrict access to this basic necessity of life for millions of poor in underdeveloped countries. Privatization will lead to even poorer health for many more people. Children will continue to die as they have only polluted water for drinking, washing, cooking and cleaning while greed and selfishness allow other people to make money.

> Water is
> From tap or well,
> precious treasure or stuff to sell.
> Clean, dirty, moving or still;
> water gives life or water can kill.
>
> © *Hannah Warwicker (aged ten when writing poem)*

There is no compassion or sense of responsibility toward people who live in fear of illness, deportation and other injustices experienced daily by so many people.

With people like Sally Thomas and Hannah Warwicker there will always be Hope.

So, readers of *Eternal Springs*, please use the writings many, many times. We have opportunities for creating and bringing hope. Hope springs eternal and hope through our actions for justice will bring life for many more people. Long may we be active. Long may we bring hope to the marginalized, deprived and terrified people who are a part of the world.

Geoffrey Duncan
May 2006

1

The Nature of Hope

Journeying in Hope

When hope invites us to a journey,
elusive, beckoning onward
but never in our grasp:
God of wisdom and promise
Give us courage to travel on.

When dreams glimmer in the distance,
fading, clouded and hidden
or shining with new brightness:
God of wisdom and promise
Give us courage to travel on.

When established patterns collapse
into the uncertainty of the unknown
and security dissolves into a memory:
God of wisdom and promise
Give us courage to travel on.

When the illusion of success
threatens to divert us
and silence dissolves into a memory:
God of wisdom and promise
Give us courage to travel on.

When we think our journey has ended
in the star-lit glow
only to find the end is a new beginning:
God of wisdom and promise
Give us courage to travel on.

Jan Berry
England

Lord of the Journey

Lord of the journey,
loosen my grip on all that might have been,
so that I may not be dragged back by regret.
Tighten my grasp of all that you want to lead me on to,
so that I may walk with you in trust and lively hope.
Amen.

Peter Graystone
England

The Door

I have taken many journeys;
some have been pleasant and predictable;
some have had the element of surprise.

I have taken many journeys;
for some I was well prepared;
for others I was not equipped.

This journey ahead is different;
I step into the unknown.
I do not know what I need for the journey.
It challenges me to walk by faith.

The door is in front of me;
I can turn away and refuse to enter;
I can ignore future possibilities.

The door is closed;
If I open it and step through,
I will experience a new tomorrow.

Nothing is certain;
But my hope is for unimagined abundance.
Open the door; I am ready to step through;
My hope carries me into an unknown joy.

John Johansen-Berg
England

Speaking of Hope ...

Who am I to speak of hope
with my wealth of green fields, blue sky,
spread of quiet starry nights,
friends and neighbours I value and trust?
For me each day is furnished with love.

When did I last beg my food,
carry brown water from a broken pipe,
make plastic sheeting my shelter,
cover my son's ears from sirens and guns,
dig with bare hands in rubble for loved ones?

– I wake up to birds singing.

Eve Jackson
England

Waiting

As an expectant mother, I wait for you.
Can I be the Lord's servant in this?
The first time it's all unknown:
woozy mornings and reflective afternoons.
Excitement mounts with passing weeks:
even when the end is in sight,
what will the last push reveal?

As an expectant father, I wait for you,
unable to bear the pain your mother must bear,
distanced by a mystery:
yet holding closer than ever,
sharing all that can be shared,
waiting for the sign to become reality.

As your expectant people, we wait for you,
unable to bear the pain that you must bear,
God-forsaken-God.
We wait for you still,
because we have heard the distant sound of angel wings,
known the silent dividing of cells,
felt unexpected love,
seen the vision of the lion and lamb:
these to us are hints of inexpressible joy.

Thanks be to God,
for cow and bear feeding together,
for children safe with snakes,
for your full round earth
pregnant with knowing you.

Thanks be to God,
for the conceived one,
the holy one,
the saving one.

Janet Lees and Bob Warwicker
England

4

It's Advent-time

It's Advent-time, our theme is hope
   in Christ who comes to liberate;
don't scan the sky with telescopes,
   but watch the here and now – and wait.

The prophets listen for the word,
   and boldly speak the truth to power;
while people think it's quite absurd,
   the wealthy quake and tyrants cower.

The Baptist in the desert cries,
   'Repent, return, for heaven's sake!'
But to the rulers, with their lies,
   he says, 'You vicious brood of snakes!'

An angel goes to Galilee,
   and tells a girl she's richly blessed:
'A virgin birth – how can this be?'
   the girl exclaims, but answers, 'Yes!'

An angel visits Mary's man,
   and calms his fears about the birth:
Emmanuel – God's cunning plan –
   to bring *shalom* to all the earth.

And so in time it comes to be:
   a baby's born who lives and dies,
he lives again for you and me,
   he comes again to dry all eyes.

Tune: Tallis's Canon

Kim Fabricius
Wales/USA

Cries of Advent

Bright Sun of Justice
burn us with your judgement.
Alive only to luxury and pleasure,
we turn to you for compassion and mercy.

Alleluia, God comes to us.

Lord of Righteousness,
save us by your grace.
Hearing the cries of those suffering from our actions,
we invite you over the thresholds of our lives.

Alleluia, God comes to us.

Morning Star,
draw near to us with redemption.
We raise our heads,
alive and expectant that your time is near.

Alleluia, God comes to us.

Patient Farmer,
sow strength in our hearts.
That resolved to live the new life,
we may do so in your enduring company.

Alleluia, God comes to us.

Branch of David,
fulfil your promise in us.
May we be rooted in your love,
flowering in justice, bearing fruits of peace.

Alleluia, God comes to us.

Janet Lees
England

6

Advent is a Time of Hope

(The Lighting of the Advent Candles)

Deep in darkness we begin,
dark outside and deep within.
Now ignite a single flame,
shadows form, let light remain.
Flaming brightly, let love shine,
flaming out through space and time.

As they gleaned the word of life,
narrative of love and strife,
people through each age have known
yet more light: God's glory shown.
Flaming brightly, let love shine,
flaming out through space and time.

John the Baptist spoke out loud,
challenged that discordant crowd,
called each one toward the light,
see it growing, gleaming bright.
Flaming brightly, let love shine,
flaming out through space and time.

Mary wondered at her lot,
blessed? Or cursed? Or loved? Or not?
Angels came and glory shone,
Feel the love, let light shine on.
Flaming brightly, let love shine,
flaming out through space and time.

Look! a star is shining there
See the stable stark and bare.
Christmas dawns, all darkness gone!
Christ has come, the light shines on!
Flaming brightly, see love shine,
flaming out through space and time.

Tune: There's a spirit in the air (if sung
omitting the chorus)

Andrew Pratt
England

Advent Peace Prayers

O Come, O Come Emmanuel

Emmanuel, God with us,
Saviour to captives and prisoners everywhere,
at this celebration of your birth
be with each lonely soul
exiled behind bars.

Emmanuel, God with us,
Saviour to prison guards and wardens everywhere,
at this celebration of your birth
protect those with power
from temptations of tyranny.

Emmanuel, God with us,
Saviour to families and friends of prisoners,
at this celebration of your birth
cheer spirits with your advent
in the darkness of every jail.

Emmanuel, God with us,
Key of David, who can unlock any door,
may we celebrate your birth
finding you again
in every lowly prison cell.
Amen.

Carol Penner
Canada

Travelling to Bethlehem

Call to Worship

We'll travel along to Bethlehem,
    a not unworthy town!
And as we go to Bethlehem
    let none of you look down
    on these unlikely people
    trav'lling this demanding way
But come with us to Bethlehem
on this surprising day!

Invocation

Ancient of Days,
    let your ageless promise be fulfilled.
Birthing God,
    let your loving labour be fruitful.
God of Grace,
    let us at last see you as one of our own.

Confession

Saving God,
    purify us
    as we turn again
    to learn self-control
    and self-giving
    from your priceless gift to us.

Assurance of Pardon

In the House of Bread God feeds us;
strength, security and peace are ours.
Jesus Christ purifies us to be enthusiastic people,
    to live our lives with hope.
We are forgiven and God's grace is seen among us.

Gloria

Glory to you God,
    who turns the world round:
    from highest to lowest,
    from great to small,
    from strong to weak,
    from shepherd to sheep.

Janet Lees
England

A Prayer for All Who are Addicted

Come, long-expected Jesus,
bringing good news to the oppressed,
coming to set your people free,
releasing us from sin and fear.
You bring good news into the lives of people
who are captive to addictions of every kind.
Good news for people who are addicted to alcohol or drugs.
Good news for people who are addicted to gambling.
Good news for people who are addicted to tobacco or food.
Good news for people who are addicted to pornography.
Good news for people who are addicted to work.
You give liberty to all who are bound.
Grant insight into the damage done.
Grant courage for first steps.
Deliver us from cravings;
let us not be led into temptation.
Let us find our strength and consolation in you.
We pray for addiction counsellors and programmes,
and for family and friends who support and encourage.
Help us to be communities of hope.
We pray all this in the name of Jesus,
who was born to set our people free.
Amen.

Carol Penner
Canada

A Prayer for Healing

Lord, you revealed yourself to Mary and Joseph
and walked with them to Bethlehem.
This Advent, we listen for your voice;
we ask you to walk with us in our HIV/AIDS-filled world.
We pray, expecting your presence among us!
Be with all who live with the effects of this disease.
Be with those who wait to die because they have no access
    to medication.
Be with children who received HIV as a legacy from their
    parents.
Be with orphans and families who have lost loved ones.
Be with countries which have millions of afflicted citizens.
Be with all who are stigmatized and ignored because they
    are infected.
Be with politicians and executives who control access to
    affordable medications.
Be with researchers and scientists who work to find a cure.
Be with healthcare workers and care-givers who comfort
    and encourage.
Lord, we hear the angel's song of peace!
Fill the hearts of people around the world with good will
as we walk the road towards justice and healing
for all who suffer from HIV/AIDS.
Amen.

Carol Penner
Canada

Deep Healing

Healing Father,
I need you near me.
Remote on mountain tops is too far away.
Come closer, come closer.

Healing Christ,
I need you near me.
The other side of the room is too far away.
Come closer, come closer.

Healing Spirit,
I need you near me.
The prayers of the Church are too far away.
Come closer, come closer.

I need you close to me:
    close to my flesh, bone of my bone,
    close to my fear, living my body life.

I need you as close as this,
    to understand that cheerfulness feels hollow
    and praise sticks in my throat.
I need you to balance the doubts I have
    alongside the faith others claim.
I need you to breathe your life into me,
    to loosen the strait-jacket of my fears,
    to support the weight of my first steps,
    to consume the anger of those who look on,
    to anoint me with your own life.
For I am immobilised by my deepest fears
    and I need to hear you say
    that my sins are forgiven.

Janet Lees
England

A Prayer for All Who Live with Violence

This year as we sing *Silent Night*
with its echoes of calm and heavenly peace,
we say a prayer for all who live in homes
where peace is absent.
We pray for children who live in fear,
whose homes are not a place of safety,
but a place of physical and verbal beatings.

We pray for seniors and other vulnerable people
whose care-givers do not care
as they are neglected or degraded.
We pray for all who are emotionally abused,
and who are not loved, honoured and cherished.
We pray for women who have had to flee their homes
or are afraid to flee their homes.
We pray for all who have been sexually violated,
and who are haunted by fear of violation.
May love's pure light this season empower us
to come to the aid of your hurting people.
We join together to sing Alleluia and thank you
for your grace that transforms our world.
In the name of the Holy Infant,
Jesus our Saviour.
Amen.

Carol Penner
Canada

Hope

We need hope for the future
in our nostalgia
for half-forgotten summer days
long past.

We need hope of pardon
in our regrets
which drift through our minds
like autumn clouds of dying leaves.

We need hope of comfort
in our fears and anxieties
fed by the long hours of darkness
in winter.

Hope of the World,
born in dark midwinter,

13

give us hope
at your coming
so that we may be newly created
with you on Easter Day.

Mary Brogan
England

An Epiphany Peace Prayer
A Prayer to the Prince of Peace

Dear God:
The newspaper brings nothing new
only an old, old story of war –
more bombing, more shooting, more bloodshed.
One more family wailing a funeral song.
Against the backdrop of brutal images,
we hear the old, old story of an angel with good news,
who brought good tidings of great joy for all people.
Angel of Bethlehem, we long to hear your song again this day.
We want good tidings for countries in crisis.
We want good tidings for soldiers caught in webs of
    violence.
We want good tidings for terrorists whose actions spread
    fear and anguish.
We want good tidings for all who grieve, and who see no
    end to grieving.
We want good tidings for children who long to inherit a
    country
where peace has blossomed.
Jesus, our Saviour,
you escaped Herod's best-laid plans.
May your Spirit of peace be born again this year
in the hearts of all who work for peace.
Amen.

Carol Penner
Canada

Reflection

There is an ancient saying that goes something like this:

For each and every one of us there is to the forefront, a host
    of angels crying out …
'Make way! Make way! Make way for the image of God.'

Catholic Women's Weekly
Australia

New Life for Old

Only the ones who were there
knew what it felt like.
One minute he was there, then gone
up into the sunlit sky,
and our hearts rose with him
so that we soared in spirit
laughing, singing, touching heaven,
and we knew something was ending
and something was beginning
and the ending and the beginning were one.
For God has gone up in triumph.

Great God of heaven and earth and all that is,
you are always with us
and we have grown used to the idea of your nearness
so that we no longer look up in awe and amazement,
recognising in wonder
that you span earth and heaven
in a moment.

As we stand in this moment
and see old plans and projects end,
new ideas and fresh understanding emerge,
help us to make the quantum leap into the new,

and understand that in the vastness of the future
and the solid familiarity of today,
your living loving presence
never ends.

Heather Pencavel
England

I Wait

In faith,
I pray,
    That justice will come.
With hope,
I wait,
    For peace to prevail.
I wait;
 I pray,
  With faith
   And hope

   Yet nothing will happen
   Until I live in love.

Richard Becher
England

German Credal Statements

We Believe in God

We believe in God.
We are not alone.
We are secure.
We are free.
We believe in the Holy Spirit, the Spirit of liberty,
    which binds us all to the all-embracing Church.

We believe in Jesus Christ,
   who reveals God to us and represents him,
   who proclaimed the kingdom of peace
   and who died because he loved us.
We believe that Jesus is alive.
He frees us from guilt, fear and death.
He helps us to live.
We believe in the God who creates and sustains the world,
   who wants us to serve him to benefit
   the world and humankind.
We believe in the living God,
   who perfects the world and renews it,
   who protects us too
   and forms us anew for everlasting life.

Joerg Zink and Rainer Roehricht
Germany
Translated by David Bunney
England

I Believe that God Can and Will Let Good Arise

I believe that God can and will let good arise,
   even out of the worst situation.

To this end he needs people who try to make the best of
everything.

I believe that God will give us sufficient powers
   of fortitude as we need them.

But he does not give them in advance,
   because we are not to depend on ourselves
   but only on him.

In such faith all fear of the future should be overcome.

I believe that God is no timeless destiny,
    but that he waits for and answers sincere prayers
    and responsible actions.

Dietrich Bonhoeffer
Germany
Translated by David Bunney
England

Gossamer Trust

Lord, sometimes I realise
that the trust I try to offer
is actually so slender, so fragile within me.

I desire it
to be as strong as the strongest tensile steel
but all too often
it's as prone to injury
as a delicate gossamer web
because the gut-feeling trust
that brings to birth the powerful 'yes' in me
battles unendingly
with the fears that make me doubt
my human limitations,
with the past experience
that jogs my memory of some previous defeat.

Earth my trust in you, Lord,
root it
in the depths of me
with unswerving surety
that you are right beside me
in every doubting, faltering, wavering moment.
That you are whispering:

here I am
let me work in,
live through
you,

let us be in this
together.

Pat Marsh
England

Live with Faith

Live with faith that speaks of Jesus,
whatever life may bring,
a faith that shows its kindness,
a hope that makes us sing,
whatever troubles face us
or those we try to serve,
whatever evil tempts us,
our faith will never swerve.

Live with joy that speaks of Jesus,
alive in us today,
a joy that knows no limits,
at work, at rest, at play.
Sing hymns to greet the morning,
say prayers to bless the night,
give smiles to cheer your neighbours
and help them share the light.

Live peace that speaks of Jesus,
a peace beyond our knowledge,
a Christ for you and me,
no weapon to protect us,
though we may share his pain,
we stand in any conflict
to make peace in his name.

Live with love that speaks of Jesus,
at work in us right now,
a love that cares for others
and does not worry how,
love that is full of mercy,
love that is pure in heart,
love that is always willing
to make another start.

Live with life that speaks of Jesus,
with purpose to the end,
a reason to be living
with Jesus as a friend,
beside us on our journey
in glory or despair,
in all that makes us human
we know that God is there.

Tune: In Memoriam

Colin Ferguson
England

Tenacity

And still it clung
and still it clung;
one lone dead leaf
which would not drop
but clung still to its branch
uncaring that all its brothers
had long ago fallen,
giving up the struggle to endure.
Why cling on through autumn gales
and winter frosts and snows?
Would spring revive it,
green it again beautifully?
Forlorn hope!

And yet I cling on still
and cling on still;
alone, as good as dead,
clinging in desperate hope
and diminishing strength
to the one who can revive
even from the dead;
clinging on through buffeting gales,
harsh frosts, sudden jolts;
clinging to the unseen hand
in fragile faith that he
will cling to me
and cling on still.

Abigail Joy Tobler
England

Mirror of Glory

'Yes,' she said, knowing yet unknowing
'How can this be?' she asks.
'Believe and it shall be done unto you.'
Trusting with joyful hope, hope against hope.
Pondering, wondering
Hidden joy, unknown sorrow.
'Blessed are you among women.
Blessed is the inheritance you give us.
Mary, you are a mirror for the glory of God.
A woman fully alive in the Everlasting Presence.'

Wendy d Ward
Aotearoa New Zealand

The Infant

She wasn't a year old, yet already at the centre of things.
The adults taking turns to remove soggy paper from her
    mouth,

tinsel fascinating her fingers, cousins zooming round about
with their new toys, beep beeping her into merry chuckles,
pausing occasionally to offer up the gift of a kiss.
One minute shrieking with delight
to be playing her part, then, silent
as snowfall at night as she catches sight
of the star at the top of the tree. Adults stop
to track her gaze, children leave their play.
The infant leading everyone to a place of wonder
on this Christmas Day.

Eve Jackson
England

When You Hope

When you hope,
what do you see?
A child's future,
a patient cured,
a friendship restored.

When you hope,
what do you hear?
The song of a choir,
the joy of laughter,
the quiet of dawn.

When you hope,
what do you feel?
The calm of trust,
the assurance of promises,
the belief in goodness.

When you hope,
what do you expect?
An answer to prayer,
a forgiving touch,
a call to action.

When you hope,
what do you do?
Commit to faith,
address injustice,
work for peace.

When you hope,
what do you say?
Challenge prejudice,
fight indifference,
speak of God's love.

When you hope,
what do you share?
The need for love,
the desire for wholeness,
the unity of all God's children.

Louise Margaret Granahan
Canada

Faith Offers the Promise of Hope

Faith offers the promise of hope
that God is all in all.
So, may Christ Jesus teach us
to hope expectantly,
that the hungry will be fed,
the homeless led to a safe haven,
the lonely and lost found,
to receive a welcome
as all are encouraged, loved and blessed.

Protector God,
stay close to all whose mission is risk,
give them continued strength
to offer compassion and solidarity,
support and shelter to the suffering and vulnerable.

23

As rejection becomes a thing of the past,
empower them in their contribution to the community
    around them.
Enabling identity and self-worth to become fully restored.

Encircle us Christ Jesus,
in the ever-widening circles of prayer
together with all the saints
that we may pray without ceasing
for courage to hope, and deliver,
healing, health, freedom and justice,
as your Holy Spirit moves among us,
uniting us, to reveal the reality of God's presence.

Wendy Whitehead
England

Thomas

Saw no hope but went
along with it, loyal
to the one I served.

Myself served by the
one I followed, how
could I not be loyal,

much as it seemed to
me certain that we
would die with him? Said:

'well, let's get on with
it, then, and do just
that.' Yes, that's what I

said and, look, I'm still
here, one of the luck-
iest men alive.

For I, Thomas, saw
him that night, in the
upper room, and count

myself, through all these
years, lucky to be
his, alive or dead.

Brian Louis Pearce
England

Living Lord of Justice Providing Hope

Living Lord
Providing Hope

Thank you for being with us
moment by moment.

Our hearts and minds know
that we are fortunate.
We have food, clothes,
a good education.

Living Lord
Providing Hope

Thank you for continuing to be with us
moment by moment.

Our hearts and minds know
we have partners and colleagues
who are far less fortunate.
Some of our friends live
below the poverty line
and yet ...

and yet ...
their generosity far exceeds our understanding.

Living Lord of Justice
Providing Hope
in your being with us
moment by moment,
instil in our hearts and minds
the will …
that determined will …
to make sacrifices
so that our friends may,
without any strings attached
or any patronising self-promotion,
be enabled to live …
to live their lives in freedom and
to know peace.

Amen.

Geoffrey Duncan
England

Transform the World

Lord our God,
in the ministry of your Son, Jesus Christ,
you showed us how to live together;
help all people across the world to seek
that sense of unity today.

In the death of Jesus on the cross
you showed us how much you love us
and your readiness to forgive.
Help us to be more ready to forgive one another today.
You brought new hope for your people
to build a better world
with a desire to work for justice and peace.
Renew this hope in people today.
Give them a burning desire
to find your peace.

26

In the resurrection of Christ
and the outpouring of
your Holy Spirit you made the disciples aware
of the power you were giving them.
Convince your people today of these same gifts
that you have entrusted to them
so that together they may transform the world.

Amen.

Edmund Shehadeh
Bethlehem Arab Society for Rehabilitation

Come Sing a Song of Faith

Come sing a song of faith,
trust in God's constant word.
Born of the Spirit's breath,
in Jesus seen and heard.
Though testing times shake our belief,
faith whispers through our pain and grief.

Come sing a song of hope,
promise for future days.
Vision and strength to cope
in life's perplexing maze.
For though we live through troubled times,
the resurrection hope still shines.

Come sing a song of love,
shown in a holy birth.
Loving so far above
all other love on earth.
A love that suffered pain and loss,
yet made a triumph of the cross.

Faith, hope and love hold fast.
Then, with God's final word,

faith realized at last.
Hope finds its longings heard.
And love will have so much to give
when with our God at last we live.

Tune: Little Cornard

Marjorie Dobson
England

On Seeing 'A Daisy' in a Frame

I was drawn like a bee to pollen
as I entered *The Gallery*. Magnified
in bold triptych glances. I stopped
nose-to-flower and rested for a second
on the fragile sense of wonder,

saying nothing –
knowing such moments can be trampled
by the smallest word,

I was a child again;
    flattening myself to the grass,
    framing with small fingers,
    excitement fluttering inside me,
    in awe of creation.

The question of perfection
too immense to carry home.

Eve Jackson
England

Cause for Joy

Deep within, the spirit searches,
looking for light, seeking peace.
The world around may seem dark
with little to encourage hope
in many situations of despair.
But the searching spirit reaches out,
makes connections, raises hopes,
risks rejection, finds fulfilment.
Kindred spirits meet and celebrate.
Their togetherness with the Great Spirit
renews, transforms and invigorates;
gleams of light give cause for joy;
a deep faith gives rise to new hope.

John Johansen-Berg
England

I Turn to You

In the dark of the night
When my demons keep me awake
I turn to you

In the cold of the morning
When the harsh light reminds me of the task ahead
I turn to you

In the bite of the wind
When my regrets eat into me
I turn to you

In the gloom of the evening
When I sit alone fearing the night ahead
I turn to you

In the blanket of night
When sleep brings me rest and refreshment
You are with me

In the warmth of the morning
When you give me hope for the day ahead
You are with me

In the breeze of a clear day
When I discern your will for me
You are with me

In the glow of the sunset
When I thank you for staying with me
You are with me

Melanie Frew
England

The Return

Light
dispelling slowly,
imperceptibly it's gone:
the darkness.

Wait!
living in darkness
the morning comes;

the Daystar
will return:
morning time.

Claire Smith
Guyana

Sight

The beauty we miss
looking
in the wrong places, wrong ways;
the beauty we miss.

The power we miss
putting limitations
on places, on ways;
the power we miss.

Grant us, Lord,
eyes
constantly open;
hearts
constantly anticipating you
in all places, in all ways –
your beauty and power,

Amen.

Claire Smith
Guyana

Rainbow Promise

You have to know where the light is
To see the promise
In the dark.
You can catch glimpses,
Without knowing.
If you stare at the dark on those caught times,
You'll see the coloured promise.
Stare.
Study.
Wonder.
Know the light behind you.
Study its source.

Then,
Each time you see the dark,
Drenched in dour and damp gloom,
Look.
With the light behind you.

Courage.
To meet the dark.

'I promise.'
'No more destruction.'
Life.
Light.

Elizabeth Gray-King
England

Sacrifice

Great and glorious God of creation, forgive us for
not loving ourselves and for misusing your planet.
Teach us each day to honour your gift of life: may
we put our hope above all in you and the new life
of your resurrection. Open our hearts that we may
understand more fully the way of your law, a law
that is not one of greed and selfishness but of self-
sacrifice, knowing that by loving others we are also
loving ourselves. Amen.

Elizabeth Smith
England

Nomalanga's Story

Sunday morning, and I'm at Nkedile School before the
start of the church service. People are gathered. They are
clustered in small groups. In one corner of the school yard
Mrs Morapedi is busy discussing issues with the members of

Manyano, our women's group. In another spot Gertrude Nleya is practising songs with the youth choir. The men are busy gossiping under a mopane tree. I move from group to group greeting in Ndebele, Kalanga and Tswana, the three languages spoken at Nkedile.

Mr Leso and I turn to the classroom where we will worship. By the door is a spreading acacia tree, lovely with yellow blossoms. A wheelbarrow is parked in the shade and in the wheelbarrow is a young girl. She is alone. Someone has brought her to church and left her in the shade while they visit with friends before the service. I go up to greet her. She's about 12 years old. She wears a pretty blue dress, no shoes; she can't walk, so she doesn't need them. Her legs are like sticks. Her back has a large hump. Her mouth is slack. Her eyes seem vacant. Nevertheless, Mr Leso and I greet her. She looks at us, but nothing seems to register.

Before I can ask about her condition, men beckon me. They want to talk with me about moulding bricks for a church building. Our conversation finishes as we are called to church. I forget about the child in the wheelbarrow. During the service there is singing, Scripture reading, preaching, praying, and then it's time for baptisms. There are 12 today. I work my way down the line. At the end of each baptism, I introduce to the congregation the newly baptized with the words, 'I present to you so-and-so, a child of God.' At the end of the line, on the floor, in a heap of tangled, useless limbs, sits the girl from the wheelbarrow.

A deacon whispers in my ear, 'We don't know who the father is, and we are not sure when she was born. Her mother is dead. An aunt brought her here. Can we baptize her?'

'Of course we can!' I say. 'Egameni lika yise, leleNdodana, lelika Moya oNgwele ...' I repeat the ancient, familiar words of baptism. I turn to the deacon next to me. 'Can we pick her up?' He helps me lift her, 'I present to you, Nomalanga Mayo, a child of God.'

'Hallelujah!' shouts the congregation; 'Amen!' they

chorus. A huge grin comes to Nomalanga. She smiles her delight at her new family in Christ. Tears spring to my eyes.

I have always had a soft spot for the outsider, the underdog. My favourite sports teams of childhood always had lots of heart, and not a lot of talent. I always felt badly for the kids at school who were a little different, kids excluded, kids on the outside. I always made it a point to be kind to them, to stick up for them if they were being picked on, something I learned from my brothers who always looked after me.

What a joy to be able to bring Nomalanga into this community of church, this new family in Christ. I am not so romantic to think that much will change for Nomalanga. She is severely disabled, unable to talk or walk. But I am encouraged by the care that someone had to bring her to church. And the hope that this church family at Nkedile will help her aunt look after her needs, both physical and spiritual for all Nomalanga's days. Nomalanga's smile as she was presented to the church, as she was the centre of our attention, is a song in my soul and heart.

This is what mission is about, bringing the love of Christ to all God's children, near and far.

Tod Gobledale
Australia/USA

God's Hands

(Ephesians 2.10)

You carried me in your hands
keeping me safe and warm,
protecting me,
moving me onward when my strength was gone.

You shape me with your hands
like the potter

lovingly forming, smoothing out the wrinkles, making me
into a vessel of honour to you,
useful for your purpose.

Yes, Lord.
Your hands are all I need.

Claire Smith
Guyana

The Word

It took a word
To set the captives free.
It took a word
To make the sick ones whole.

One word
One man
One evening
One available man
Patiently sitting
Until they were whole –
All.

Who will be that one?
Who will say that word?
Who is available
Patiently
Sitting
Until they are whole –
All?

It takes
One person
One word –
Available.

Claire Smith
Guyana

Sunrise – Sunset

At the rising of the sun, Lord, we stumble into your light.

As the dawn unravels and reveals new horizons, we step
out hesitantly, unsure of our footing yet determined to
move on.

So it is with our faith.
New understanding dawns, our spirits lift and enthusiasm
fires. We discover new perspectives on life.

Lord, help us never to forget those first steps of faith and
the promise they offered.

—

In the sunlight, nature is at its best. Colours shimmer,
flowers display, birds sing and perfume fills the air. Until a
cloud casts shadow and the scene darkens.

So it is with our faith.
Father, in the light of your Son we too can step out and
grow, filling the air around us with light, colour and sound.
We display your creative love with the creative spark you
have placed in each of us.

Lord help us to remember the sunlight, especially when the
clouds begin to gather and our faith falters in the darkness.

—

At the setting of the sun, nature settles for sleep, quiet
comes and shadows lengthen. Colours blaze briefly as day
ends.

So it is with our faith.
Lord, there are times when we need a resting place, a quiet
time when we reflect and fold into our faith as the silence
and darkness enter our lives.

Lord help us to trust in you as you guide us in darkness,
comfort us in silence and meet us in the shadows. Show us
how to stand firm in our faith, whatever happens.

Marjorie Dobson
England

The Movement

When God moves
earth and heaven stand still
in awe at the artistry of orchestration
stilling time and space,
fusing disparate paths and goals
into one unified chorus of your will be done.

When God moves
the unlikely meets the unlikely in unlikely times and spaces
leaving indescribably beautiful awe-
filled moments of grace and peace and healing.

When God moves
the spirit moves
and reality shifts into difference
. . . and yes,
the sun rises upon a new day
as the Spirit breathes and hush,
the Son appears.

Ah!

Claire Smith
Guyana

A Celtic Pilgrimage

I come in faith to Lindisfarne
Wild, windswept home of
Centuries of spirituality.
I seek a space; a time to be with God
To calm fears,
To face necessity,
To muster strength.

But the day is cold
A quick coffee to warm the hands
Some postcards to write
(So much better sent from the island itself)
A shop full of celtic wares that wear a celtic grin.
Books to browse, present to buy –
(So near to Christmas now).

And now to commune with the sea and sky
To taste the wine of Cuthbert's heritage.

But the day is grey
A visit to the vinery to taste the mead
Several bottles will make handsome gifts
Interesting tee-shirts for children and pleasant chatter
The celtic patterns wearing thin.

And now to the shore, the waves and the birds
To find where God speaks loudly to those who have the
    ears to listen.

But the day is wet
It's time for lunch and
Delicious soup with fresh coriander
(What would Cuthbert be doing with fresh coriander?)
Home-made bread; a warm-hearted waitress

A cashier who waits while an old woman counts out
    pennies
And time to read some pages of the inevitable book.

And now at last to the craggy sealine
Fortified to face the long-awaited time with God.

But the day is short
In just an hour the tide will be in
The causeway will not be passable
I must think of leaving.
Time for a quick walk to the headland
Looking down on the Priory –
Seat of Celtiana.

And suddenly I am caught by the
Loudest, wildest wind
Deafening my ears
Upsetting my balance
Seizing my weight in its strong arms.
I feel in my bones
The holding, intensifying, frightening majesty of God
And I surrender to its power.

In those last minutes of our frantic lives,
Squeezed in as the tide turns
God comes to where we are
God comes to our greatest need
And holds us fast.

And it is good.

Carole Ellefsen-Jones
England

Lord of the Evening

Colours of evening
paint the sky,
open my eyes
to see
beyond myself.

Sounds of the evening
still my soul,
sharpen my ears
to hear
within myself.

Peace of the evening
embrace me now,
draw me closer
to yourself.

Lord of the evening
meet me
here.

Pat Marsh
England

2

When Life Seems Hopeless

Hopelessness

Where do you find hope
when there is no bread for today?
Where do you find hope
when you have lost your family?
Where do you find hope
when the world seems not to care?
Hope is challenged
by every form of suffering,
by every friend who forsakes you,
by every prayer which seems unanswered.
Yet hope has the habit of continuing,
like a still small voice
which refuses to be silenced by the storm.

John Johansen-Berg
England

Not So This Christmas

Did shepherds once guard sheep
on hills near Bethlehem,
fearing only wild animals?

Not so this Christmas –
when the danger that lurks in the hills is a camouflaged
    tank.

And were those shepherds made fearful
by bright lights which turned out to be angels
and a loud noise which became
a heavenly song to the glory of God?

Not so this Christmas –
when the sound in the sky is the roar of helicopter
    gunships,
the light, the bursting of a deadly rocket.

Did shepherds once walk freely
from those hills down to the town
where folk slept soundly – apart from that group in the
    stable?

Not so this Christmas –
when the route is blocked by checkpoints
and a towering concrete wall,
and citizens, walled in, fear for themselves and for their
    children.

Is that family still there – poor, vulnerable?
Mother, father and the child
who will know suffering and sorrow and death,
yet through it all, bring hope.

People of God, go afresh to Bethlehem
in the light of reality.
Occupied then – occupied now.
Innocents slaughtered then – and now.

Go and see the child who will grow
to be the man who cries for justice,
who dies to bring new life.

He invites us to follow him.

Wendy Ross-Barker
England

Hospital Corners

It's been a long shift and he's very heavy
For such a little man
Little and old. Turn over John, don't
Make such a fuss. We're only making your bed.
It's my wife's birthday and she's dead.
Don't cry John – we don't have tears
On this ward.

Heavens, she must have died years
Ago. Why is he *still* crying? Surely
He must have got over it!

There you are, John. Your bed's made now
All you have to do is lie on it.
Don't think we don't understand, we all
Have our troubles, there's no need for tears.

Roger Grainger
England

May the Light of Justice Shine

When people are denied dignity of name and culture:
abused, ridiculed or subtly excluded;
where race or class or gender
are used to deny rights and liberty:
God our hope and our deliverer,
shatter the rod of prejudice
and let your light bring freedom to our darkness.

Where the prosperous profit from the poor
and families are caught in the spiral of debt;
where men are deprived of work and role
and women's labour is underpaid or invisible:
God our hope and our deliverer,
shatter the rod of prejudice
and let your light bring freedom to our darkness.

43

Where the strong bully and harass the weak
and the vulnerable are exploited and abused;
where war breeds cruelty and torture
and leaves hunger and homelessness in its wake:
God our hope and our deliverer,
shatter the rod of prejudice
and let your light bring freedom to our darkness.

Jan Berry
England

Poverty

I was hungry for the Word of God
and was left hungry.
Lord, have mercy.

I was thirsty for the living water
and was left thirsty.
Lord, have mercy.

I was a stranger craving love in God's house
and was left a stranger.
Lord, have mercy.

I was naked lacking the armour of God
and was left naked.
Lord, have mercy.

I was in prison needing a Saviour
and was left in prison.
Lord, have mercy.

Sir, we would see Jesus
but we saw him not.
Lord, have mercy.

Harry Wiggett
South Africa

Doing the Impossible

Start by doing what's necessary;
then do what's possible;
and suddenly you are doing the impossible.

St Francis of Assisi
Italy

Hopeless or Hopeful?

How hopeless it feels to still witness prejudice

How hopeless it feels to still hear righteousness
in the name of a God image

How hopeless to witness reaction with violence
instead of response with understanding

How hopeless it feels to witness so much projection,
not removing the plank from my eye before
I can take the speck out of the other

How hopeless it feels to know today is the same
as it has been throughout the ages.

Can the New Story spread in time?

Can the Sacredness of all be known?

Can we know the same 'Ground of Being'
connects us all?

Yes?

Then I am hopeful.

Eleanore Milardo
USA

45

When Hope Is ...

When hope is trampled
by the bulls of injustice
and the hordes of hate,
I pray to you, imprisoned one,
    caught,
    tried,
    condemned,
    speechless.
As you hang there,
may we hang on.

When hope is buried
by the mounds of apprehension
and the grave diggers of fear,
I pray to you, buried one,
    anointed,
    wrapped,
    entombed,
    silent.
As you lie there,
may we keep vigil.

When hope is vulnerable
to the weight of suffering
and the gales of grief,
I pray to you, rising one,
    breathing,
    moving,
    recognising,
    naming.
As you are there,
may we greet you.

Janet Lees
England

46

Mary with John

'I bore him but to see
him dead by thirty-three.

Who knows the grief, the loss,
to see him on the cross.

Joseph, I'd long since lost,
he being older than most.'

'Would you have borne him had
you known what waited the lad?'

'Ah, that's an old one, son!
How can I, or anyone,

know what's in store for a wife?
Trust, love: laugh, cry, that's life!

Trust God, who gave the child,
to know it's cried and smiled.

Ask not what is the plan,
but love, trust, while you can.'

Brian Louis Pearce
England

For Survivors of Abuse

Did I see you?
When I was hungry you broke bread with me.
When I was sick you sat by my bedside.
When I was in prison, you petitioned for my release.
When I was sexually assaulted, you listened to my pain.
When I was afraid to be alone, you stayed with me.
When I felt guilty and ashamed, you told me it was not my
    fault.
When I had to go to court, you went with me.

When I was filled with anger and hatred, you did not reject
   me.
When I was filled with sorrow and hopelessness, you held
   my hand.
When I kept my story secret for years, you understood
   why.
When I called on God for help, you came and helped me.

Carol Penner
Canada

Runaways

Searching Love, we pray for runaways.

We pray for those who have to run away,
because their parents treat them cruelly,
because they are in impossible debt,
or because they are persecuted for their faith.
   May they find life in you.

We pray for those who run away from truth or pain,
who will not admit that someone they love is gone for ever,
whose agony builds inside.
We pray for those who cannot stand their own weakness,
not even long enough to ask forgiveness.
   Forgive them all,
   help them to forgive themselves,
   and help them gently to the place
   where they will see reality.

We pray for those of us who run away from you:
from the challenge of your words,
from your demands of discipleship,
from your love.
   Thank you for your persistence,
   searching us out with love.

And for those whose running leads to a worse place,
who fall into darkness
like the belly of Jonah's whale,
who fall under the lash of the storm
or crawl under railway arches.
    We ask for confidence in you,
    that they may find peace
    and homecoming
    in your presence.

Bob Warwicker
England

Hope Comes in the Morning

When the land is dry and barren
reduced to degraded dust,
wait for God to restore life,
bringing growth for our emptiness.

Wait, wait on our God.
Keep vigil, keep faith,
for hope comes in the morning.

When the city is derelict
with boarded-up windows and abandoned cars,
wait for God to restore its vitality,
bringing anger to our numbness.

Wait, wait on our God.
Keep vigil, keep faith,
for hope comes in the morning.

When we are numbed with grief,
raw pain breaking the monotony,
wait for God's tender touch
bringing comfort to our healing.

Wait, wait on our God.
Keep vigil, keep faith,
for hope comes in the morning.

Jan Berry
England

When the World Appears to be Against Us

When the world appears to be against us
Father of Jesus, bless our love with strength
to support each other in any storm
and listen only to our hearts.

When we are misunderstood and hated
Father of Jesus, bless our commitment
to be who we are meant to be
and to refuse to retaliate in kind.

When we are reviled, sneered at, or shunned
Father of Jesus, bless our care for each other
that we may continue to smile
and to face the future arm-in-arm.

When we are smeared and denigrated
out of fear and ignorance
Father of Jesus, bless those who stand against us
and hold us safe in the knowledge
of all we mean to each other.

When we are used as a threat to children
and considered a risk to unity, health and morality
Father of Jesus, sanctify the deep wells within
and turn us in peace to your love
that will take us on.

Duncan Tuck
England

Lichen

As lichen clings barely to stone walls,
gaining scant nourishment or foothold
yet surviving barrenness tenaciously,
so I cling to the stone-hard side of God,
finding little support for my little strength,
little comfort for my empty hope.
And yet I cling.

The lichen grows so imperceptibly
only passing aeons note the change –
as only eternity will show the progress
I have made towards that union with God
that transcends mere desperate clinging,
to become a loving embrace of two
into one.

Abigail Joy Tobler
England

A View from the Edge

Why should I,
how should I have faith
in a figure from history?

These fables of a star,
sages, angels,
a babe and mystery …

What are they to me in this place?

There are tales of miracles
like the water turned to wine,
parables that teach obedience;
old stories from an ancient time …

How could these imbue belief?

And this figure you call 'Son of God'.
(I've found no proof – so do not know.)
This man met a violent end,
as have many …

Who reveres them now?

You will say this man came to life
a second time and is alive …

Christian, I cannot believe this
just because you do.
I have tried.

And if I should believe …

What difference then?

I read, I look but I do not find.
I listen … the words are hollow.
All words are empty where action
does not with confirmation follow.

I need to fill the void within.
I'm sick of life on the margins.
I seek something real and lasting.
I'm sick of life that is no life,
in a world that is insincere …

But this Jesus, this 'Christ' of yours,
does not come here,
he isn't real …

And life's not real
and isn't worth the living.

Jessica Hope Isherwood
England

Pandora's Lament

The black hole of despair draws me to the edge.
I see the headlong, hopeless, flight of the dove,
Diving to avoid the raptor's claw.
The whirring wings become the beat of my frantic heart.
Barbed wire binds tight my brain,
Each act of treachery gouging deep,
Close knotted with the lost and lonely.
Gnawing grief in a tumult of tears,
Pools into fetid swamps of hatred,
That burden and suppress the spirit.
My creamy skin suppurates with sores,
As mankind's depravity bursts forth in stinking pus.
Then I see a small child, holding a dock leaf.
Gently she soothes and binds my wounds.

Rose James
England

Demanding God

You ask of us
what we clearly can give
only sometimes.
You demand our faith
and time
and hope
from a sea of DNA that is hopelessly flawed.
We are stupid and petty
and jealous and mad,
worldly and innocent
brave and crazy
brash and dither.
In your image?
Am I?

Alma Fritchley
England

Prayer for Male Survivors of Violence

God of Comfort:
We pray today for men and boys
whose lives have been scarred by abuse and violence.
We pray for boys bullied and molested
by people who should be their friends.
We pray for boys sexually abused and exploited
by people they trust who should protect them.
We pray for boys who cry their tears alone
with no one to comfort them.
We pray for men who have suffered physical assault
and have fear as a constant companion.
We pray for men who have been sexually assaulted
and who are not allowed by our society to name their
    victimization.
Jesus, teach our Church to see your face
in all men who suffer from the effects of violence.
Amen.

Carol Penner
Canada

Desert

You have dwelt long within a desert place.
In the blue caves of thought behind your eyes
you keep the hurt that people throw there.
Your words pick up the spears and when you speak
they sometimes wound me.

I will try to pull them free,
and in brown woods of thought
they will melt into tears;
and when they fall secretly
perhaps they may in some strange way
water the dry places of your hurt.

Something may overgrow
to heal.

Cecily Taylor
England

Humanism

Religious dogma keeps Iraqi women out of sight,
probably figuring out what to eat next, while the men fight.
Political strivings put American women on the front line
ready to risk capture or death,
or become the star of a Hollywood extravaganza.

Like the clash of cymbals, these disparate women
are brought together in the theatre of war.
Westerners expressing freedom of choice.
The other women hidden and covered
because of their men's religion.

Is it a vain hope that these women
could share their common humanity?
Discover themselves reflected
in each other's eyes.
Finding mutual desire for peace
and striving to live, become, beget.
Over a cup of tea.

Wendy d Ward
Aotearoa New Zealand

Grief in Iraq

I woke from sleep, the night was dark and still,
The silver moon shone on the window sill,
My dream had been of children in Iraq,
Of mothers wracked with grief, all dressed in black.

Their children played no more, for they were dead,
'We did not ask for this', their mothers said,
Such terror they had never felt before,
Their children and their homes destroyed by war.

Their hatred for the men of war was real,
Men trained to kill, their weapons made of steel,
What right had they to make their children die,
To launch their obscene missiles from the sky?

Far from Iraq, the men of power sleep well,
They won't admit they made a living hell,
Blind to the tears the grieving mothers weep,
Unmoved by human sorrow, fast asleep.

John Stephenson
England

Humane

Did you see the marine medic?
Chubby and bespectacled
holding the Iraqi child
traumatized by war.
Did you see the tender
puzzled look on his face?
The enemy whom he had come
to defeat and liberate.

We, onlooking, can only guess
at his bewilderment.
Cradling this wisp of humanity
caught in the crossfire of greed and cruelty.

If there are any rags of hope
to be gleaned from this benighted war.
It is in this image of a soldier
sitting cross-legged in the dust.

Vulnerable, ambivalent,
sharing the simplest of human needs
to touch, hold, be held.
Friend or foe?
Who is the vanquished now?

Wendy d Ward
Aotearoa New Zealand

Prayer Against Violence

Perfect love casts out fear
and so today we pray for your spirit of love on our world.
Cast out the strapping of bombs to bodies.
Cast out the explosion of bombs in crowded places.
Cast out the tricking of children to carry bombs.
Cast out the desperation that leads people to terrorist acts.
Cast out the making of walls that divide and imprison us.
Cast out the firing of missiles and the bulldozing of homes.
Cast out the prejudice against people of a certain race or
     culture.
Cast out the political structures that perpetuate violence.
Cast out the hatred that produces fear.
Send down the courage to reach out in peace.
Send down the resolution to not return evil for evil.
Send down the creativity to find peaceful political solutions.
Send down the wisdom that politicians and diplomats need.
Send down the commitment to work together to end
     terrorism.
Send down the power of non-violence to create change.
Send down the comfort and justice that victims need.
Send down the love that will end our fear.
We ask these things in the name of Jesus, the Prince of
     Peace.
Amen.

Carol Penner
Canada

Children Die from Drought and Earthquake

Children die from drought and earthquake,
    children die by hand of man.
What on earth, and what for God's sake,
    can be made of such a plan?
Nothing – no such plan's been plotted;
    nothing – no such plan exists:
if such suffering were allotted,
    God would be an atheist.

Into ovens men drive brothers,
    into buildings men fly planes;
history's losers are the mothers,
    history's winners are the Cains.
Asking where was God in Auschwitz,
    or among the Taliban:
God himself was on the gibbets –
    thus the question: Where was man?

God of love and God of power –
    attributes cannot be squared.
Faith can face the final hour,
    doubt and anger can be aired.
Answers aren't an explanation,
    answers come at quite a cost:
only wonder at creation,
    and the practice of the cross.

Tune: Scarlet Ribbons

Kim Fabricius
Wales/USA

Sudanese Refugee Helps Others

Prince Manyiel Deng from southern Sudan last saw his sister-in-law more than 20 years ago before he fled to Khartoum after government troops shot dead his father and eldest brother. She was in very good health.

When they were reunited in early 2005 she was emaciated as were her four sons and a daughter. Her face betrayed signs of suffering after more than a decade in a refugee camp in north-western Kenya.

Mr Deng, who lived in Egypt before going to Australia as a refugee in late 2003, confesses that he avoided her initially, as he was so distressed by news of relatives dispersed by the civil war and famine which had claimed two million lives and displaced twice as many people.

After finally meeting with his sister-in-law, he has asked the church to help him pay rent for 24 ailing children of his relatives who live in Nairobi and to assist 15 families in a refugee camp to migrate to Australia.

John Ball
Australia

Refugee, Refugee, Grow in Hope

The refugee frets endlessly;
All is unfamiliar;
All is fraught with strangeness;
Memory is grim and sharp;
Security and survival now measurable
in host country situation with just process
and compassion clearly shown.

Yet refugee frets endlessly
too traumatised to hope
that new life is possible;

that transition will redeem horror;
that health will blossom;
that refugee will become naturalised citizen
known by personal name
happily well-integrated, memories eventually healed.

The seed of hope needs nurturing
in refugees' hearts
to strengthen trust in
God's care.

God bless the hope sowers.
God bless the hope growers.
God bless the refuge providers.
May sanctuary truly become the home
in which all are known by name
and not by sad condition.

Glenn Jetta Barclay
Aotearoa New Zealand

Prayer in Response to the Rwandan Genocide

Transforming God:
take my anger,
and make of it a wellspring of compassion
for the bereaved and distressed;
take my revulsion,
and make of it a burning desire to overcome wickedness;
take my incomprehension,
and make of it an open channel
through which I may see the realities of evil;
take my pity,
and make of it a source of remembrance;
take my despair,
and make of it a fountain of hope:

Turn me, O God, from indifference and apathy
that I may work to ensure that never again
will the sanctity of human life
be destroyed in this – or in any – way.

Chris Chivers
England

Reflections upon Ramallah in Poetic Form

My Key Your Key

Refugee, you hold your key
Near your heart.
The key that belongs
To your old home's door;
The key to your original place.
Your key means hope to you.

Refugee, you cement your key
Onto your present shelter's wall;
The key that belongs
To your old home's door;
The key to your original place.
Your key means faith to you.

Who fills your old home now
With family space?
Who has had new keys made –
Had your locks replaced?
Will they exclude you for ever,
You, the forced-out one?
Their key brings despair to you.
For their key is no longer new.

Glenn Jetta Barclay
Aotearoa New Zealand

A Communion Hymn in Time of Moral Famine

Can this our bread be living bread
If all the children starve?
Unconsecrated, underfed,
As prophets lose their nerve?

Can any vine shed saving wine
With power to redeem,
When lips that share the cup consign
Flesh, blood to low esteem?

'For if you feed a hungry child
You feed – are fed – by me':
A simple message, now defiled
By power's perfidy.

Forgive our meagre Eucharist:
Can sacrament suffice
That feeds on famine's holocaust
And mocks the bread of life?

God, send new prophets on the winds
To claim the cross instead
Of those who vaunt her twisted ends:
Command the stones be bread.

Tune: St Flavian

Edward Moran
USA

I Don't Really Comprehend

(Trying to understand my relationship with those with disabilities)

I don't really comprehend
the way you think or what you say;
but you are a child of God
blessed with love, within God's sway.

Valued for the hidden grace
you do not know, you cannot show,
grace that's hidden from my eyes
grace that God can realise.

So I'll value you my friend;
each day I'll seek to understand:
how to learn and share with you,
take my learning from your hand.

Then together we will grow,
together we will reach for hope
far beyond our wildest dreams,
yet within God's boundless scope.

Tune: Metre 7.8.7.7

Andrew Pratt
England

Face to Face

I met her yesterday
inwardly weeping.
You could tell
the depression weighed heavily.
Conscious of the lone silence
she spoke to break the barrier of pain.

I prayed
for the Spirit's anointing
to refresh and renew
mysteriously as morning dew.

Treasure the developing space
to be free
to become.

Simply draw up a chair,
share – face to face
with the only one
in whose image you're made.

Dig deep:
hold nothing back
in times of doubt and stress
it's good to talk, watch, wait and listen
to one who knows you well and longs to bless
while you prepare for ultimate wholeness – given.

Wendy Whitehead
England

Six Angles on Depression

(A series of reflections on surviving depression, with echoes of Holy Week,
Easter Saturday and Ascensiontide)

Like a Stone

Dropping
like a stone
to the bottom
of a dry well,
or
plummeting
like a lift

in a concrete shaft;
I am in free fall,
my stomach rising
into my throat
and falling back
through the soles
of my feet.

Dragging
a carcass
up a steep hill,
or
struggling
to find air
underwater,
the tide rising;
my brain is fuzzy,
and voices echo,
as if in a dark cave,
as I look for
the energy to
reclaim my life.

Anger

A gradual
or sudden
build up
to a heart-pounding-
skin-flushing-
head-screaming-
mouth-bursting-
bowels-purging-
words-failing-
tears-streaming-
all-consuming
anger.

But it's unfair.
The process of selection has been used before ...
But it's unjust.
The minutes of the meeting state ...
But they don't reflect the silences, the unspoken and unspeakable,
the tension and dissent that dare not be named.
Having consulted widely we have decided to ...
But that is not what the community wants.

Anger that causes the pitch of my voice to raise up several
tones and tenses my larynx as I try to spit the few words I
have from the place they are lodged at the bottom of my
belly to take up some space on the silent floor of this
encounter.

Anger that has my head whirring as I try to find a word or
phrase and weigh it for appropriateness whilst still dealing
with the numbness that has hit my chest and the fire that is
raging in my bowels.

Anger that has me alternately swearing and using words
from the fringes of my vocabulary in a vain attempt to
communicate the unspoken obscenity of what is
happening.

What happens to me
happens to others.
What happens to others
happens to me.
A meeting is not just
a place where things are said.
It's a body place
where silence plays
as big a part
as words.

Hope

It was Hope brought me here;
her firm grip and eager stride
urging me onto our next adventure.
Since then she has aged alarmingly.
I have watched her struggle
as her physical and mental capacities
have begun to slide away.
Now, as with every step,
she gasps for breath,
her dishevelled appearance
a sign that memory and thought
are in full flight.
Some days she perks up,
looks around her
ready for anything,
but most often I wait
in the corner of her room:
will she die today?
There are no more harp-filled songs.
The trees are bare and seem unlikely to leaf.
If Hope dies, I wonder,
can she rise again?

The Shroud

A shroud descends
before its time,
wrapping tightly round,
blotting out the sun.

As it wraps taut,
be still and breathe:
remember the sun
rising behind clouds.

Greet life newborn,
bare in winter;
spring will come again,
sloughing off the shroud.

Not Here

His body is not here.

There is a body here,
but it's not his.
At least, I don't think it is.
It claims his name
and has some residual features
that suggest a family likeness
but it's not his.

Besides which, this body
is barely alive.
It hardly breathes,
it scarcely moves,
it struggles to remain conscious
at all of the world around.

So where is he?
Lost, decades back,
centuries even,
by continual cell division?

Or did he, like so many,
just get up and leave,
when it all got so deathly?

As I stand gawping
at the gaping tomb,
I wonder where to look first.

Blue Sky

Blue sky
is hard to imagine
on days when drizzle
dampens everything,
or when low clouds
blunt the edges
where earth and sky meet,
so minds cannot expand
nor dreams soar upwards.
When ice crunches
underfoot,
it is hard to risk
a skyward glance
to check visibility.
The earth sucks boots down:
it grounds us.
The clearest day
can be shaken
by bits and pieces
burning up in the atmosphere,
raining down on car parks
and back gardens,
reminding us
to keep our heads down.
Only one who knows the skies
inside out
can be companion
in the drizzle,
propelling us skywards
even without a thaw,
to risk the burning,
breath-taking,
lung-bursting
gasp of recognition

that sets us on
our next adventure.

Janet Lees
England

From Dependency to Self-Reliance

It used to be asked:
What is mental illness?
What can we do for mental illness?
What can we do about mental illness?
But these are yesterday's questions.

Today's question, the question that matters, is, What could a person with mental illness, empowered, do for him/herself? Today the call of the new innovative strategies and pragmatic approaches are required not only to combat the stigma surrounding mental illness but also to engage people in productive work, by providing opportunities, whereby they take charge of their own destiny and find their own voice as partners not as petitioners in the community development process.

The requests of the person with mental illness

I have only two requests.
I do not ask for money
although I have need of it,
I do not ask for medicine.

I have only two requests,
all I ask is
that you remove
the road block
from my path and give me an opportunity.

Clearly money and medicine are important, but the essential and enduring truth that should be highlighted are surely the

70

rights of the people to have an opportunity to show their hidden potential and be self-reliant!

Anil K. Patil
South India/England

Remove the Roadblocks

Caring Christ
prompt us
to hear the pleas of the people
who are living with a stigma.

Caring Christ
motivate us
to act for people who are valuable
as individual human beings.

Compassionate Christ
free us from our hesitancy
to walk with the unknown,
to enable people to be
      empowered and
to become
      self-reliant

Compassionate Christ
liberate us from the status quo
so that we will
      act
      campaign and
      remove roadblocks
for the people
(of whatever age)
who are dispossessed.

Geoffrey Duncan
England

Hope for All God's People

Introduction

Children are the group most vulnerable to poverty. They rely on adults for the provision of basic needs. The number of children living in poor households is heartbreaking and these children can be disadvantaged for life.

Good News

Jesus' message was designed to bring good news for all the people of his time but only by being in the first place good news for the poor.

There has been much research on the meaning of 'the poor' in the time of Jesus and on the precise economic and social status of the first Christians. In this reflection I want to point us into the direction of a group in the church in which I serve as a minister. The group called Responsible Christian Citizenship (Church and Society) serves the poor in a community situated about 20 kilometres from the church. From time to time, we set up a soup kitchen in that area and we feed most of the community's children.

The Invitation

On one occasion I invited a non-active, non-committed member of the church to come along with us to one of these soup kitchens. Early on a winter's morning we left to set up a soup kitchen in the community.

I noticed that my friend brought his Bible along and I indicated to him that this is one of the days on which the biblical text is not necessary. What is important, is the way we are dealing with the children and members of the community. That will speak louder than the text. It is your actions and knowledge of the Bible that counts.

A Five-Year-Old Girl

A five-year-old girl caught his attention on that morning. Standing in the cold with no shoes, no adequate clothing and her body shivering as the frost bit into her feet. When he handed her the nice and warm cup of soup, she took it with so much thanks and appreciation that tears filled his eyes. For the next ten minutes the little five-year-old treasured the cup of soup as it warmed up her body from the inside. 'You can have another cup of soup', my friend promised the little girl. 'Yes please, Oompie' [Uncle]* she said, 'I would like to take it to my three-year-old brother.' 'Where is he?' my friend asked. 'He is at home', the little girl replied. Leaving with her on that cold winter's morning changed his life for ever. On his return, he told me about the appalling circumstances of the family.

The experience brought the best qualities out of my friend and today he freely shares his testimony with everyone. God has touched his life.

Today he is retired due to ill health, and this former Financial Director of one of the big steel companies, situated west of the City of Gold (Johannesburg) became a committed member of the group and the local church. Blankets, food parcels are on a regular basis distributed in the community and soup kitchens always feature on the group's agenda. My friend's vehicle is well known in the area. The gospel of Jesus Christ changes people's lives and brings hope to people in their different circumstances.

God is at Work

God works in wonderful and miraculous ways, and through the small efforts of church groups and individuals, God brings hope into hopeless situations. The gospel is always good news for the poor. This is part of the shape that any message must take if it is to be in truth the gospel. We must stop preaching abstract truths and vague generalities that are supposed to be equally applicable to everyone but, in fact, are good news to no one.

Any preaching of the gospel that tries to remain neutral with regard to issues that deeply affect the lives of people prevents change. It is a watered-down gospel and it will fail to bring hope into a situation of hopelessness.

Oompie – Afrikaans term which means Uncle
(One of the official languages in South Africa)

Kelvin Harris
South Africa

I Asked

How am I to find hope
in this much sadness?

I see no flicker of light
and have wearied in darkness.

As each hour flowers
I cannot catch the colour
or hold its shape.

Mere moments leave me numbed.
Some days staring outwards
blinds me with brightness.

Trudging through the mundane
has helped me survive
the very ordinary of life – for a while.

Now, I find myself digging –
there is nowhere to go
but the very depth of my soul.

And slowly surfaces a treasure.
Guilt overwhelms. I question. Should this be mine?
But it shines and keeps on shining.

A small voice inside speaks of this as my future.
It grows out of my need to live,
nourished by the love of those around me:

Gifts of faith;
kind acts, prayers, unselfish thoughts.
God's love as simple as a smile.

I know my life will grow, flourish
with wonderful memories and new discoveries.
Morning waiting to be picked.

I also know that some days will not bear fruit.
But in me somewhere is hope
and, given time, this will open into joy.

Eve Jackson
England

Where is God?

Where is God when lives seem pointless,
  kicking empty cans about?
Where is God if they're avoiding
  homes that always shut them out?

Where is God when people queuing
  for a brew are short of change?
Where is God when airborne bottles
  find their human prey in range?

Where is God when desperate addicts
  rob the weak of rings and pride?
Where is God if life in prison
  teaches yet more ways inside?

Where is God when single parents
    meet eviction in the face?
Where is God if youths who struggle
    are not given time or space?

Where is God when racist taunting
    turns the fear in 'us' on 'them'?
Where is God if half-truth tabloids
    make us foolishly condemn?

Where is God but in each question,
    in the prompting us to care
how our lives might start to answer
    those who ask 'Is God still there?'?

Graham Adams
England

Lost Hope

I cried for lost hope.

It wasn't that it was wonderful
hearts and flowers romance.

It wasn't remembered birthdays
or unreminded anniversaries.

It wasn't even moonlit
walks in autumn crisp-cool air.

It was hope.

It was hope that this man of
reality
would be the man of my
dreams.

Then, you see,
the shock of honeymoon-learned
reality
could be lived with.

It was hope that died.

That's why I cried.

Elizabeth Gray-King
England

Hope Is Always There

Listening God, you hear us when we cannot speak,
when despair and turmoil leaves us faint and weak.
In love you call us back to you again
and your grace reminds us how you feel our pain.

Searching God, you find us when we go astray,
as self-centred living takes us from your way.
In love you seek us, show us what we've lost,
and your tears remind us what forgiveness cost.

Suffering God, you lift us from our deepest grief,
when emotion blinds us to our own belief.
In love you touch us with your nail-torn hand
and your wounds remind us why you understand.

Risen God, you show us love too strong for death.
Evil deeds defeated by your living breath.
In love you teach us never to despair,
your new life reminds us, hope is always there.

Tune: Noel Nouvelet

Marjorie Dobson
England

Just Call Me Martha

It was the look of surprise that was a surprise to me – or should I say looks, as I saw it more than once. These people know me! Why are they taken aback? They had surely noticed that I had not been to church much lately, not done my usual work on the website, missed meetings and social engagements, so why should it come as such a surprise when I said that I'd been off work for three months with depression? It is the middle-class ailment of choice in this day and age. It can affect anyone. It does affect over a third of us.

So why didn't they realise? OK, they know about a successful professional career, a happy marriage, a suburban semi-detached dream home with no money worries and, of course, an active church and social life. No cancer or sick parents. The perfect life.

The career. I hate it.
The marriage. Under pressure.
The house. Window dressing.
The work for the church. Just call me Martha.

Melanie Frew
England

Prisoners of Hope!

(A Reflection on Zechariah 9.9–12)

This was the Bible reading we were due to use in my church on the Sunday following the suicide bombings in London, 7 July 2005 … a passage celebrating the one who is to come on a donkey and on the foal of a donkey … yes, apparently on *two* animals, which Matthew's account of the 'triumphant entry' fulfils … but how ridiculous it sounds! Imagine it, this 'triumphant' entry – no Messiah coming in glory and honour; neither in secrecy; but very publicly, and very bizarrely, bringing about justice and peace through a very different method – the protest of a clown.

Zechariah exclaims, 'O prisoners of hope!' and we heard that cry on that day, feeling like prisoners, trapped by fear, silenced by explosions, desperate for some signs of hope. How we are indeed prisoners of hope – people, churches, communities imprisoned within our mindsets and world views, within the limitations imposed upon us by our fragile self-esteem, confidence and power, within the structures and ideologies of a society at war with itself – and yet still we have hope.

But our hope is rooted, not in the images of wealth or force, celebrity or beauty projected by the news media, but in the protest of a clown – the one who comes to us on a donkey and on the foal of a donkey, a ridiculous figure, a distraction and a nonsense. Our hope comes to us, not as we expect nor even as we hope, but it is such an object of derision who makes real change possible … the possibility of a new quality of community where, ridiculously, enemies are loved, the poor are given God's kingdom, and we dare to be *for* people no one else will dare to be for. O prisoners of hope, take heart!

Graham Adams
England

The Silent Cry

Does anyone care
that I sit and stare
and wonder why
I'm here at all?

A still small voice
whispers – yes – rejoice!
You're a precious stone
in my kingdom's wall.

Harry Wiggett
South Africa

Where are the Mathematics of God?

Breach The Wall! is the call.
Stop all breaches of human rights
imposed by The Wall.
For The Wall breaches human rights.
The Wall must be breached,
broken and removed. The Wall must fall!

Block the bombers! is the cry.
Stop suicide bombing caused by martyrdom, despair
and rage.
Suicide bombing denies human rights.
Suicide bombing must be discouraged, prevented,
denounced.
Suicide bombing must totally stall!

Israelis say that The Wall is to block
Suicide bombers coming their way.
The bombers say that The Wall and the Israeli Military
ensure more
suicide martyrs.
A terrible equation.
Read it backwards or forwards,
The elements remain the same.
Wall equals Suicide bombing.
Suicide bombing equals Wall.
Will it ever change?
For zero equals zero.
No Wall equals no suicide bombers.
No suicide bombers equals no Wall.
Your cause equals our effect.
Your effect equals our cause.

When will the mathematics of tragedy be transformed?
Shalom equals Salaam.
Salaam equals Shalom.

Peace equals Peace.
God's mathematics.
Simplistic? Unrealistic? Hopeless?
Not when God is in the equation.

Glenn Jetta Barclay
Aotearoa New Zealand

Unwed Mother

So lonely
with her life-full bundle
clutched like treasure
to her breast
she only seeks acceptance
where she's heard
that she'd be blessed by God
and by forgiven sinners
loved because
for grace and love she came.

But all she found were
pointing fingers
not to Jesus not to his cross
but to a man-made loveless ledger
gaining cents – for her, dead loss.

And sadly as she turns away
the lack of love she longed for
leads her more astray.

Harry Wiggett
South Africa

Song of Resistance

(re-making the news)

God, in this world of confused misconception,
wondering whether what's wrong may be right,
help us expose what is evil deception
causing its victims to give up their fight.

God, we would join with your praise of persistence,
daring to find ourselves judged by 'the least',
raging with your kind of gracious resistance,
drawn to your *pro*test, whatever 'the beast'.

God, in the face of what's true by perception,
broadcasts selectively making the news,
help us tune in to your wisdom's reception,
testing the wholeness of edited views.

God, in the midst of poor people's subsistence,
helpless while rich countries reap what was sown,
may we uncover and share your insistence –
'power to the people to eat what they've grown!'

God, as we perpetrate cycles of violence –
contracts for weapons bound up with our 'aid',
people next door suff'ring neighbourly silence –
help us re-view and denounce what we've made.

God of this world and its longed-for salvation,
help us as sisters and brothers to grow,
breaking the forces maintaining starvation,
building your new kind of world from below.

God, we who share your Anointed One's story,
finding what's human defined by 'the lost',
help us pursue your brave, vulnerable glory:
love that is boundless whatever the cost.

Graham Adams
England

How I Wish

How I wish to turn the clock back;
everyone could change their mind
to travel in by bus or tube
or never be there at all.

How I wish the smoke would clear now
and there would be no bodies,
casualties from a twisted hell
many names placed on a list.

How I wish you'd never parted,
never left and never lost
sister, mother, daughter, lover,
or the baby she once was.

How I wish they'd all stop talking
of the Blitz and how we won,
or the spirit of the people
when you're quite broken, empty.

How I wish they would stop saying
that you're lucky to survive;
that 'times heals' and 'you'll get better'
when you've left that self behind.

How I wish I had the answer
when life's completely broken:
limbs were severed, minds were shattered
all at once, there's no way back.

How I wish I had some words now,
standing here just speechless, numb:
placing flowers in the garden
I can't say we'll rise again.

How I wish you didn't have to
make that journey every day,
crowded in like many cattle
rattling down that iron track.

How I wish that all bus drivers,
passengers and passers-by
didn't have to stare so wary
at every brown bearded face.

How I wish there could be peace now
between everyone worldwide.
Not that echoing eerie silence
of the inside of the train.

What I wish is much more painful,
something to work at each day;
embracing our varied neighbours,
learning how to hope again.

Janet Lees
England

An Eye for An Eye

An eye for an eye only makes the whole world blind

Mahatma Gandhi
India

Letter to Dominic and Gregory

London, September 2002

My dear sons, it is nine o'clock in the evening and, as your
mother relaxes for the first time in the day, you are at last
asleep. I have just sneaked into your bedroom to see you,
Gregory, curled into the corner of your cot – clutching those

little pieces of rag you carry with you all the time – and you, Dominic, gently hugging the teddy which has been yours since you were three months old. It is a picture of indescribable beauty but for some reason, tonight, it is also a picture that fills me with foreboding.

My fearfulness seems to date from the time the other day when you, Greggy, slipped on one of the rocks which surround the sand pit in St James's Park, and when you, Dom, your face filled with tears, ran towards me to tell me that an older boy had destroyed the 'tower' made of sand you had spent 20 minutes patiently constructing. One day, maybe I'll be able to explain to you these first experiences of the downside of being human. Since, teetering on that rock, Greggy, I saw the many times in the future when your life will brush with danger – physical, emotional, psychological. And in your face, Dom, I saw the look of a much older man crushed, as we all are, by the insensitivity of others.

Of course these images jostle constantly with other more positive ones. I marvel at your extraordinary ability to put sentences together, Greggy, just as I am astonished at your ability, Dom, to remember so much of what you experience. But for reasons, some of which seem far beyond my control, all this has been clouded of late.

A few weeks ago two little girls were abducted and killed in a quiet village in Cambridgeshire. Their senseless deaths have caused thousands of people to feel anger, sorrow, even despair. They were just playing near their homes one minute and the next they were lying in some ditch naked, mutilated and lifeless. In the days following their abduction, like many people I was caught up in their story as all of us hoped and prayed they would be found alive. But the night their corpses were discovered I found myself clinging to the two of you even more tightly than usual at bedtime, wondering what kind of a world your mother and I are protecting you from or preparing you for.

And now as I gaze at the two of you all I can see is the empty beds, mattresses, bits of floor which must haunt so many parents the world over tonight. Parents in the townships on the Cape Flats whose children have died of AIDS. Parents waiting a year ago on September 11th, clutching pictures of their older sons and daughters, hoping they would walk out of the wreckage of the Twin Towers and be back as usual to put their own children to bed. Parents somewhere whose terrorist sons' choice of 'death for a cause' must by now seem inexplicable or hollowly heroic. Parents in the villages of Afghanistan whose children were playing in the streets one minute and crushed under buildings the next when homes were blasted to smithereens in retribution. Or, what is worse, perhaps parents the world over who must watch their children die the slowest of deaths through lack of food, water, education and opportunity.

All of which means that I am fearful of letting you go into that big world out there with all its dangers. But as I continue to stare at the two of you, I also know that I must do so because real life always comes at a cost.

This is a truth I re-learnt a few days ago when I was standing in the ruins of the old Coventry Cathedral – the one I described to you which was bombed during the Second World War. I was standing looking at the great cross made out of charred beams of wood that they found the morning after the bombing raid. And as I looked so I heard again the first screams you let out, the ones that gave us the overwhelming news that you were with us – and also let us know that you were fed up with the hard work of being born! This reminded me that all life begins with joy coming out of pain. That's just the way it is.

And if one day you can piece all that together I hope that you'll also feel, as I do, that it's worth struggling to believe – and live by – the truth my moment of epiphany contained. For while there's no getting away from the horrors of the world – about which, sadly, you will learn more and more each day; and there's no avoiding the hurts and pains you will suffer as a human being – awful though that is for your mother and me to contemplate; your smiles, your laughter, your playfulness, your questions, your openness, your sheer love of life, the thought of what you might do – what you already do – to make the world a better place, all this lifts my spirits each and every day. I think it offers the only certainty there is, which is hope itself.

Chris Chivers
England

God of Understanding

I've hated you
and loved you
and been disappointed in you.
As you no doubt in me.

I've looked for you
and you've been absent.
I've yearned
and quested
and you've been curiously quiet.

Did I look in the wrong places?
The wrong faces?
I've defied you
and denied you,
Thrice and thrice and thrice again.
Peter never had exclusive rights!

And no longer
the absentee,
that still small voice
has become a shout
a yell
I can deny no more.

She is insistent
And persistent
And my heart opens for Her.

Funny, I mislaid my faith.
But She never did.

Amen.

Alma Fritchley
England

3

Spirit of Hope

Good News!

Praise God for good news – bringing hope to the poor!
Give thanks that the Spirit of God dwells in each one,
offering freedom for prisoners,
renewed insights,
relief from disease or oppression.

Rejoice in the spirit of hope!
Wherever Christ's love shines
through selfless love of volunteers,
tending the sick,
binding the broken,
risking all
in the face of extreme poverty,
famine or drought.

God of all hopefulness,
protect all who minister your care,
your healing,
your everlasting love.

Thanks be to God.

Wendy Whitehead
England

Our God Shall Be a Shelter

Our God shall be a shelter
With arms that open wide
When hearts become a welter
Of wintriness and pride.
Incarnate, God is homeless,
A refugee for love
Evicted by a promise
From habitats above.

God comes to us a stranger,
No room nor inn nor bed.
Rude dreams brought forth in manger,
Rood wood beneath his head.
See Mary, Joseph stealing
Through streets and hearts all iced
Toward habitats appealing
To carpenter and Christ.

God's likeness takes on glory
When struck in human flesh,
Though bitter be the story
Of cross athwart the crèche.
How can the people trust us?
With hammer, nails and wood?
Let's turn these tools to justice
And build a world of good.

A world of many mansions
With lives and loves unique
Fulfilling God's intentions,
Embracing slave and Greek.
A world where none are homeless
Where love alone runs wild,

A habitat of promise
For lion, lamb and child.

Tune: Angel's Story

Edward Moran
USA

Hope (1)

Hope is the power inside you
Hope is always true
Hope will always abide with you
Hope will always be inside you.

A world without hope
Would be a world of sorrow.
No dreams, just pain.
Goodness would be crushed
and evil would triumph.
The world be lost in anger and strife.

My hopes are
To live a life of happiness
    Not of strife;
To follow the path of truth
    Not of lies;
Do my duty as a citizen,
    Contribute to society;
Be loved by animals, family and all.
They are my hopes
Remember them well.

Martin Edwards
Aged 10
England

Into the Unknown

We pray for those who go reluctantly into the unknown –
an elderly woman leaving a life-long home for a flat in
    sheltered accommodation,
a man being made redundant from the work that gives
    stability and identity –
no choice but to go; into a future unchosen; hope the merest
    gleam.

God of the unknown
Walk with them and show them the way.

We pray for those who go with relief into the unknown –
a woman leaving the familiarity of violence and the
    struggle to survive,
a refugee escaping torture and prison for an uncertain
    existence in a strange land –
leaving behind the past, for a future hesitantly unfolding
    into a new growth.

God of the unknown
Walk with them and show them the way.

We pray for those who go joyfully into the unknown –
a man resuming study, finding new confidence in the
    excitement of learning,
a woman taking up a new post, eagerly responding to the
    challenge,
stepping forward into a future bright with possibilities
    and the
fulfillment of dreams.

God of the unknown
Walk with them and show them the way.

Jan Berry
England

The Gift of Hope

We give thanks for the faith that grants us light in darkness, to see divine love at work even through suffering.

Help us to hold fast when hope fails and understanding is dimmed, ever to trust in Christ who brings new life out of death.

Raymond Chapman
England

Circles of Hope

Come together in a circle.
Make them all around the world.
We need to have connection
to tell our stories of truth.

The Spirit of Wisdom encircles,
touches each, one by one.
Come, sit and listen,
strength of connection
is in the ring.

Makes no difference what religion
we are all the children-one.
The spirit of truth is sure to spread
from circles all around.

Eleanore Milardo
USA

Sing for Harmony

Tell it in the valleys;
announce it on the hills.
The time of peace is coming.
There are those who readily resort to violence

to maintain justice
or to help the oppressed.
But those who take up the sword
also perish by the sword.
Violence begets violence
in every generation.
Observe the women in black
who witness to peace in silence;
see men from many cultures
who protest non-violently for justice.
Children of all nations
sing for harmony.
The message from God
comes across the mountains
announcing good news of peace.

John Johansen-Berg
England

Hope, the Phoenix

Hope has a strange habit of rising:
Sometimes like a kite
Wind-soaring skywards
Above our limitations,
Only to crash upon the stony beach
Of disappointment.

Sometimes like a tree
It burgeons into blossom
Blinding with its brilliance
Intoxicating by its perfume
Only to wither and shrivel in storms
Of disillusion.

Hope has a strange habit of rising:
Just when you think that in dust

It lies buried and dead
It will stream from the dark earth
Of your soul and lift it
On wings of fire.

Christine Ractliff
England

I Am The Living Vine

O Holy One, help us see
your down-to-earth presence
made human in Jesus of Nazareth
   as your living vine
   rooted in you, rising in him
   and branching in every human.
Show us through your vine
how we can transform
   our fisted outrage
   into your hand outstretched;
   our trampled wasteland
   into your oasis;
   our 'Country-Club' churches
   into your 'Community Centre';
   our eye-for-an-eye and
      listening-with-only-one-ear
   into your turning-the-other-cheek and
      attuning-the-other-ear.
O Holy One, through your vine help us root
   our internecine/intercontinental world
   in your self-giving love
   that it may blossom as
   your interconnected world.

Norm S. D. Esdon
Canada

I Am Greater than My Thinking

I am greater than my thinking
Or the follies of my heart
I can grow in self-awareness
Which promotes a brand new start.

> For I trust the Spirit's oneness,
> Trust the way compassion cares,
> Trust the lifeforce, trust the wholeness,
> Trust the love beyond my fears.

I have found connecting pathways
In my joy and in my pain.
I can dwell in myst'ry's wonder
Far beyond all thought of gain.

> For I trust the Spirit's oneness,
> Trust the way compassion cares,
> Trust the lifeforce, trust the wholeness,
> Trust the love beyond my fears.

I will sideline self-importance
I will sing though full of grief,
I will rise from dismal moaning
Like a spring-time shoot or leaf.

> For I trust the Spirit's oneness,
> Trust the way compassion cares,
> Trust the lifeforce, trust the wholeness,
> Trust the love beyond my fears.

W. L. Wallace
Aotearoa New Zealand

A Body Prayer

Thank you for our bodies
for new baby bodies,
for young bodies,
for middle-aged bodies,
for old bodies.
Thank you that we are somebody in your sight.
Thank you for beating hearts,
for blood which carries what we need
and takes away what we don't.
Thank you for bones and muscles.
Thank you for memory that hides inside us,
and points us to you.
Thank you for our church body
and the body of Jesus,
broken for us, raised for Your glory.
Amen.

Carol Penner
Canada

Laughter in Her Eyes

Hope is for my daughter –
for the music in her fingers
and the laughter in her eyes.

May she go gently on her way,
in tune with children,
an engaging companion,
generous with time.

Let the scars that she carried not wound again.

May she live
to delight in a world

into which she brings
compassion and integrity;
the warmth of friendship,
and the rainbow arch of joy.

But if long-fingered shadows
invade her day
may she find resolution
through the touch of human healing
and in the deep places
where soul enfolds soul in silence
and hope is the last-broken cord of love.

Jill Jenkins
England

I Met You in the Most Unexpected Place

You were in the tears of the young father
    the love for his child in the incubator.

You were in the laughter of the grandmother
    the joy of seeing her grandson for the first time.

You were in the sleep of the baby
    the peace of innocence and youth.

You were in the arms of the nurse
    the patience to feed one so small.

You were in the thoughts of the schoolchildren
    the kindness to raise money for the ward.

You were in the prayers of the congregation
    the faithfulness to support the family.

You were in the hands of the doctor
    the humility to care for the weakest.

You were in my heart
　　the self-control keeping a mother from breaking.

Melanie Frew
England

Those Who Can't Speak Will Shout

Lord of all,
We pray for your people who cannot speak yet shout to
　you in a loud voice.
Lord, give us ears to hear their shouts when we cannot hear
　their voices:

　　The bruises of cowering children that shout the need for
　　　rescue from abuse and neglect;
　　The blank faces of despair that shout the need for hope
　　　and vision in a crushing world;
　　The emaciated bodies that shout the need for food in a
　　　selfish greedy world;
　　The silent terrified faces that shout the need for justice
　　　and peace in an oppressive world;
　　The defiant courageous faces that shout the need for total
　　　religious tolerance and freedom for your word to be
　　　heard in every land.

Lord, help us to know how to respond to what we hear and
　to act upon it.
May our lives shout to give you praise and to give witness
　to your truth.

Maureen R. Davis
England

Robin

I step back and I circle again –
a dance, a ritual. My neck craned.
The tune repeats just out of reach
like a butcher/baker boy refrain
already a whistle up the next street;
his roundelay delivering all kinds of hope,
fancying his chances in his bright waistcoat.

Eve Jackson
England

Litany of Thanksgiving
A Journey of Self-Acceptance

I started life as a quiet child, often afraid and unsure of who
I was meant to be. I had little self-worth. Over the years a
great many people have touched my life in a healing way
and so I give thanks.

I give thanks for the many counsellors I've met, who have
listened, advised and helped me over patches of deep
depression.

I give thanks for the Samaritans who were there for me, and
are always there, whenever anyone needs a friendly ear.

I give thanks for the person who told me about process
therapy and recommended a therapist.

I give thanks for that therapist who enabled me to move
beyond my pain into a place of action, enabling me to hear
my true voice and teaching me to love that true self.

I give thanks for the vicar who accepted me as I was, even
in pain and anger, and simply loved me unconditionally.

I give thanks for my children who gave me hope in times of
darkness, and continue to be there in my life.

I give thanks for my acupuncturist who used her skill to bring my scattered emotions together and who taught me to use my body to connect with life through Chi Gon.

I give thanks for my spiritual director whose guidance on contemplation has helped me so much in my search for self.

I give thanks for my partner of the past four years, who has brought stability and happiness into my life.

I give thanks for the child I once was, who had the courage to stand up for herself, despite the cost, and I love her.

I give thanks for Jesus, an unwavering light, even though at times I was too blinded by tears to see.

I give thanks to God, beside me, within me, for me ... beyond all knowing, yet ever present.

I give thanks for all who helped me make the long journey from the dark place of childhood abuse and adult depression into a place of joy, hope and freedom.

Sarah Ingle
England

I Am Strong

A shower of barbs and arrows
pierce my heart when I witness
injustice.

You welcomed all at your table.
You accepted everyone,
   marginalized,
    oppressed,
     women loved into wholeness.

In quiet,
my heart fills with your
healing voice
'I approve you.'

I am, no longer co-dependent
in an institution addicted to power.
I have a new voice of courage
to speak,
whatever the risk.

Christ led me to this place.
I can speak when confronted
no matter what the consequence.
I am strong!
I feel the grasp of Christ's hand.

Eleanore Milardo
USA

In My Silence

In my silence the truth persists.
You may not deface it.
In my silence your shame endures.
You may not erase it.

In my silence is my power and my defence.
You cannot put lies into a mouth
that does not utter words.
Nor can you trap one who refuses
to answer your taunting.

In my silence is my strength,
while I have strength enough
to bear it.

Anon

Strange Tongues

I cannot read music.
Those lines and dots
and strangely curving symbols
are merely patterns
filling up a page.

I cannot play music.
Black and white keyboards,
stringed instruments
and tubes of wood and brass,
are dead in my hands,
silent to my lips.

I cannot sing music –
not with any confidence.
My lips frame words.
My voice sounds tuneless
to my own ears
and I am wary
of letting others hear
my faltering efforts.

Music is a foreign language to me
and I am as incompetent in that
as I am in other tongues.

Yet music moves my soul
and I listen and am carried
by its haunting power
into a world, alive and beautiful,
and the music speaks
in a voice all its own.

The Spirit's language
is a foreign tongue,

not understood.
And yet it speaks,
controls and liberates
and moves
into the deepest areas of the soul
to make a moving music
of its own.

Marjorie Dobson
England

Thought ...

It strikes me that Jesus could be seen as not only the first industrial chaplain but also as the first trade unionist.

He visited local industry, fishing, agriculture, the council, retail, pubs and clubs and city centres where he not only listened but he challenged and negotiated ...

Better pay, better conditions, equal opportunities and a whole lot more.

I'm fairly convinced he would have been standing on the picket lines during the miners' strike, the fire fighters' strike. He'd have been on his Harley (in my life Jesus is a biker) during the fuel crisis and yes, he'd have been on the Meadows in Edinburgh in July 2005 raising awareness of poverty issues in our world.

But what am I saying? When Christians gather in solidarity to fight injustice of any kind he is already there ... in us and in those we meet.

Cate Adams
England

Trade Union Prayer

Lord we pray for those who work daily
in the struggle against oppression,
inequality and injustice in our workforce.

For the shop stewards, who, working
alongside their comrades, need to be
aware of all sides of the argument.

Help them to be humble in their listening,
tenacious in their negotiating,
creative in their thinking and
Christ-centred in their doing.

Protect them from the hurt and
misunderstanding of prejudice,
free them from petty squabbles and
insignificances so that they may focus
on the real issues of today's society
with clarity and understanding.

Save them from bullying, from mistrust
and anxiety, grant them a clear vision
and a thirst for justice, not power.

Amen.

Cate Adams
England

I Will Give You Hope

An orphan child,
Unwanted
Uneducated
Unwashed

Diseased
Distressed
Dying.

Move me to action, Lord
I shall see the truth
I will learn more
I give my time
I will share my money
I offer my prayers
I will tell your story.

Child of God,
I will care for you
I will educate you
I will wash you
I will treat your illness
I will calm you
I will give you hope.

Melanie Frew
England

Blessing for Parents

We pray today for a blessing on parents;
    two parents in one home,
    two parents in two homes,
    single parents,
    extended family caregivers,
    foster parents,
    and all who are in a parental role.
Give patience when love wears thin.
Give tenderness even in the face of anger.
Give clarity in the face of difficult decisions.
Where financial resources are stretched and anxiety reigns –
    bring relief.

Where there is estrangement and discord between parents
or between parents and children –
bring your peace.
Where illness and disability pose special challenges –
bring renewed energy.
Dear Mother and Father of us all, inspire us with your love!
Amen.

Carol Penner
Canada

A Prayer for Playing

As children, as young people, and as adults
we thank you God for time to rest and play!
Help us to choose activities in our leisure time
that re-create us and diminish no one.
Tune into TV programmes with us.
Listen to music with us.
Surf websites with us.
Play sports with us.
Party with us.
Watch movies with us.
Enjoy our hobbies with us.
Read magazines and books with us.
Be a guest in every chat-room we frequent
and a spectator of every game we play.
We invoke your presence as
Emmanuel, God-with-us, this week as we play,
in Jesus' name.
Amen.

Carol Penner
Canada

For Moira

She stood.
Dark squarely heavy
rooted to the floor, feeling for safety.

Clear adept eyes
directed inquiry through thin shining specs.

The eyes caught titles on my shelf.
Skipped this one, held there,
sauntered over that one.

Her body, yet safely stable,
allowed her hand, stretching,
to match eye catch.
Is this the One? one of?

(She knows/holds a pain.
A big pain, made of little accumulations
and one endlessly memorable violation.
The pain still violates;
robs bare the dignity there;
still violates, lays waste the dream wait;
memorable Violation
forever altering direction.

She holds a pain.)

The bound words might touch,
identify, reach, dignify –
the volumes might violation verify.
Another's words might speak hers.

She stood,
dark squarely heavy
rooted to the floor.

Elizabeth Gray-King
England

Sometimes a Word Surprises ...

I smiled at my computer screen
yet not foolishly
for floating on its dark terrain
was the word 'Salaam'
in clear three-dimensional angles;
the colours of which
changed from gold to soft green, teal to blue;
apricot then on to grey; to canary; to ivory
and back to gold again.
'Salaam, salaam' it proclaimed as it danced with a
strange kind of calligraphic dignity.

'Salaam' – the word shone bright
gliding on, not unlike
an ice skater
moving in graceful flow and turn
on the rink of my screen.

How is it that I have
'Salaam'
thus inscribed?
Perhaps
it is a natural consequence of residing
within Palestine
for a considerable time.
Peace becomes salaam.
The dance of the angels.
Hope of the nations.

Glenn Jetta Barclay
Aotearoa New Zealand

Words of Waiting

Waiting – we've all experienced it …
    waiting – felt in so many varieties …

Anxious, fearful waiting – when a loved one is late or
   missing
     or when the diagnosis is uncertain

Agonising waiting – for the pain of suffering to be
   relieved …
     pain of body, mind or spirit

Frustrating waiting – when the plumber is delayed or the
   train
     is late or the expected letter has not yet
     come or when they say 'I'll 'phone you
     back', but never do!

Desperate waiting – when there seems to be no hope of
   relief
     and the suffering is unbearable

Resigned waiting – believing that nothing can be done to
   bring
     change for the better

Sad waiting – for the one who knows that death is
     approaching and for close ones standing by

Boring waiting – long, tedious hours on watch – bringing
   exhaustion

But change the tempo,
change the tune – raise your spirits
focus afresh on the waiting that points to better times …

Hopeful, excited, expectant waiting –
          a dear friend is awaited,
          a celebration is planned,
          health is restored,
          war will end
   – peace and reconciliation are on the horizon

Wait – be ready and active …
     for joy and goodness, life and love are never destroyed
     and can awaken hope.

Wendy Ross-Barker
England

Island of Hope

I'm sitting in the meeting hall of the World Council of Churches in Geneva, Switzerland, listening to Pacific Islanders speaking about the difficulties they face and the hopes they share. Theirs is a liquid continent covering a third of the world's surface; with 176 million sq km of sea and 10 of land; 2,500 languages and dialects; 25,000 islands with only 20 percent inhabitable. I hear the words, 'We people of the Pacific are prone to being marginalised on the international stage.'

Climate change is real and not theoretical. Fifteen island states in the Pacific are vulnerable. The impacts include: rising sea levels, king tides, coral reef destruction, loss of coastal land, change in rainfall patterns, increasing severity of cyclones, loss of crops, loss of drinkable water, and threats to human health. I hear these words: 'The people of the Pacific are crying for their islands and homes and don't want to be forgotten.' The Kyoto protocol is heralded as a milestone but then I'm reminded that the USA and Australia have not signed up, and there's a need for even stricter legislation on greenhouse gas emissions. Where then are the signs of hope? In a range of local responses; in education on the issue; in commitment to ecumenical collaboration; and in churches in other regions acting in solidarity with the Pacific.

HIV/AIDS is a major concern. There are 9,000 reported cases in a population of 66 million in 22 Pacific Island nations. Papua New Guinea has 7,320 of these cases in a population of 4 million. A young man from Fiji shares his personal journey of life with this disease. He tells of his fear of rejection and death; his marriage being threatened; his going bush for 18 months. Where are the signs of hope? In the transformation of people's attitudes to those living with the disease, and in raising awareness about and advocating on issues of HIV/AIDS in congregations and communities.

The Pacific Islands have been a nuclear testing ground for almost 50 years. In all there have been 332 tests: by the USA at Bikini Atoll, the British on Christmas Island and the French at Mururoa and Fangataufa Islands. Consequences have been the relocation of people living on those islands and adverse health effects for islanders working at the test sites, including cancer pathologies. Where are the signs of hope? In efforts to raise up the voices of victims so they can be heard, and in applying pressure for action to be taken against those responsible.

Finally I hear these words: 'We've taken you to the Pacific and presented you with the hopes and dreams of our people. We need action, and more importantly, we need solidarity from our Christian brothers and sisters.'

Pacific Island churches say they are united in their hope for the realisation of the kingdom of God on earth, especially in the Pacific. Though there are many islands, the hope which unites them makes them one 'Island of Hope'. The image of the Island of Hope is of people together braving all the adverse circumstances they face.

John Roberts
Aotearoa New Zealand

Where There is Good News

This mother lost her children
in the genocide.
She could so easily
have fallen into despair.
That was not her way.
She gathered a group of orphans,
deprived of their parents
in the killing spree.
She gave them a home
and a mother's love.
In a dark place
she was a source of light.
In a time of despair
this was a moment of good news.

John Johansen-Berg
England

Miriama

I watched her, charmed
by her royal dignity
and look of cool command
her innate grace
as she attended a young woman's class
to learn English
with other virgins of her race
within the confines of a Ramallah Refugee Camp.
Her noble stance and glance
were not contrived
or consciously sought.
A long line of superior breeding
was natural to her demeanour;
was in
her seventeen-year-old face.
Intriguing to observe.

113

From whence had she come?
What genes were hers?
For she was a delight; an unexpected delight.

I photographed her
recording those eyes so remote, so seemingly knowing,
as if brooding from forebears' ancient seeing;
her lips part smiling, part dreaming;
head-cover similar
to that of her ancient sister.
I am glad that I caught her thus
for Miriama,
responding foolishly, as young girls are wont to do,
with an attentive lover
acted inappropriately
for her faith and culture –
this quite recently.
In terror she fled as far as Hebron
from her home in Ramallah
from her enraged brother.
Miriama was found, brought home in disgrace
amid family shame.
'She will be killed,' said her virgin friends.
'Her life must surely cruelly end.'
Miriama may already be slain.
I am devastated.

As for me, I wish I could
rewind the film
re-capture dignified Miriama
recording her for ever in her bloom
to remove the stain of impulsive youth
from family memory.
To reveal the truth
the royal truth.

Ah, but this time there is a miracle of forgiveness.
Miriama has been given another chance.

'She made a mistake, forgive her' said the Camp Director.
'Let God's love reflect here.' Miriama lives on.
Perhaps peace and justice is possible in Palestine.
We have hope, always we have hope.
Cultures can and do change.

Glenn Jetta Barclay
Aotearoa New Zealand

Prayer of Remembering and Confession

Leader: We remember all who are held hostage …

All or Voice One: **All who are held hostage by history or by people bearing arms; by politics based on a balance of terror, by their own fears and prejudices.**

Leader: We remember families who are separated and people who are exiled from the place of their birth …

All or Voice Two: **People separated and exiled by frontiers, by barbed wire, by division in the minds of men and women.**

Leader: We remember places long held as holy by people of different faiths …

All or Voice Three: **Places which have become territory to be fought over, places of joy which have become places of *suffering*.**

Leader: God, we pray for reconciliation.

All or Voice Four: **God, you show us the meaning of reconciliation in the life of Jesus Christ, through his touch, his words, his actions, which reconciled people to you and to the community.**

Leader:	God, renew us, that we, too, might be reconciled with you and others.
All or Voice Five:	**Empower us to be agents of your reconciliation with a touch, a word, or an action.**
Leader:	We proclaim your power, O God, to reconcile.
All or Voice Six:	**We pray for your realm to break into our lives.**

Amen.

Tod and Ana K. Gobledale
Australia/USA

Communion

Leader:	We praise you, Nurturing God, for feeding us at Christ's table here and all around the world. Patiently you plant the seeds of faith, waiting to harvest the fruits of our lives. Busily you grind the grains of our experiences, mixing the dough. Quietly, restlessly you yeast Christ's church to life.
All:	**Bread of the world, in mercy broken.**
Leader:	We thank you, Nourishing God, for the strength we draw from the shared witness of our sisters and brothers who partake of this Holy meal. Make us bold to seek justice, and quick to act in compassion. Shape us well that we might become the Bread of Life to those who need us.
All:	**Fruit of the vine, in mercy shed.**
Leader:	We rejoice in you, Surprising God, for your abiding presence. Spark our imaginations that we might share your dream of reconciliation and unity. Open our hearts so Christ's healing love may flow from your gathered church into a parched, thirsty world.
All:	**Let this feast of yours remind us.**

Leader: We pray to you, Healing God, that your people find sustenance at Christ's table. Feed our spirits that we might work together as the body of Christ around the world: preaching good news to captives, restoring health to those in pain, reconciling those who are estranged.

All: **That by your grace our souls are fed.**

Distribute the bread and juice.

Prayer of Thanksgiving

Leader: Almighty and loving God, we marvel at the privilege at eating at Christ's table. Made one with Christ in the fellowship of this meal, we know ourselves to be at one with all your people everywhere. Help us to express Christ's reconciliation to all we meet.

All: **Amen.**

Tod and Ana K. Gobledale
Australia/USA

Hope (2)

Thirteen years have passed since my Deed Poll for Change of Name was signed, sealed and delivered to me. Legally I had a new name. A name of my choosing. I had 'absolutely relinquished and abandoned the use of my former names and in substitution thereof adopted and formally assumed my new name'.

I had chosen Hope as my second Christian name. My middle name. I had placed Hope at my centre. I had chosen my new name and cast off my given name along with the many other labels my damaged and damaging parents had attached to me.

Hope was at my centre. Hope of recovery. Hope of a life. Standing up and demanding a new name was a watershed for me. One way of moving beyond damage. I was opening into life, a gift from God. I had hope of a worth-while future. The way to move into that future was to believe that I had already received God's gift. I had to live life believing not just that life could be mine, but that it was mine. I would live believing God had already given me this gift and that healing was assured. For that is HOPE.

Hope is at my centre. Now I have a life. I discover more of it and more about it daily. Life has become a good experience with its mix of joy and sorrow, giving and receiving, dreaming and creating, community and solitude. Hope has brought me to this alive place. I live in Hope – I always will. Hope will take me into Eternity.

Jessica Hope Isherwood
England

and accompanied by this prayer:

O God, whose nature and name is LOVE,
who watches over all your children,
knowing each one by name
and numbering the very hairs on their heads;
thank you for the compassion and care
you have shown to those whose parents or carers have let
    them down;
thank you for the strength and support you have given them,
to help them hold on to life and hope;
thank you for their courage in speaking out,
which puts so much of our silence to shame.

Thank you for the challenge of their stories,
calling us to watch over all your children
with tender and loving care;
to call to account all who abuse their trust,
and to call in question all who would turn a blind eye.

Jean Mortimer
England

Be Kind to Yourself

(in five easy steps)

1. Approve of yourself unconditionally – the whole of your identity, creativity and imagination, are unique to yourself. No one can take these away from you and yet, paradoxically, it is the same for everyone else. Recognise your strengths and the achievements you have made in life. Be kind to yourself, stop being so critical and judgemental and whenever possible give yourself a treat. Why not? You deserve a treat just as much or the same as anybody else.

2. Love yourself unconditionally – we all love our families, friends, relatives, possessions and pets – for goodness' sake have some love for yourself. If you always focus on the need to be loved, then you are missing out on basics. Fire comes first and smoke comes later. Don't start off with smoke and expect fire to be created. Why? Because our heart is like a musical instrument. If it is not used, it will not strike the necessary chords, so what's the point in having the musical instrument. When you have a quiet moment or in bed at night, in your mind tell yourself that you love yourself – it's easy, no one else can hear you. When you look in the mirror tell yourself that you love yourself and it will bring a smile to your face. If you do this regularly, you will see the difference!

3. Forgive yourself unconditionally – everyone in life has at some time or another done something (or many things) that later they wish they hadn't or disapproved of. These are mistakes that we have all made; everyone makes mistakes and they are a normal part of being a human being because we learn from our mistakes. The biggest and worst mistakes we make are usually the ones from which we learn the most. Remember, the person who has never made a mistake has never learned anything.

4. Accept yourself as you are, unconditionally – you are not perfect and neither is anyone else who walks on this

earth, so accept all your weaknesses and imperfections just as you are.

5. The commitment for growth for yourselves – you have to keep this commitment, otherwise things don't just happen. Understand that we are all seeds and the seeds have to become trees. If you die as a seed, you haven't lived up to your purpose and experienced the true quality of your life. Become aware and keep up the commitment for growth. In the name of service, do not forget yourself. In serving yourself, do not forget others. With time all is possible.

Anil K. Patil
South India/England

Fundacion Solidaridad – Teresa's Story

Arpilleras – the bright, handmade pictures created with thread and scraps of cloth – are very much a part of Chile's history. Women began making them in the 1970s when General Pinochet was in power and it was difficult for the ordinary people to let people outside Chile know what was happening.

Today, making the arpilleras provides a valuable income for many women in and around the Santiago area. They sell their handicrafts through Fundacion Solidaridad, which has been helping to develop handicraft workshops since 1976.

Teresa Cerda travels into Fundacion Solidaridad's offices in Santiago, about 50 kms away, to bring in the finished work and collect the orders for her group.

'I am a widow. A few years ago, my husband died of cancer. The money from the arpilleras was extremely useful then. I received a widow's pension, which was very small, so it was important for me to have extra income for me and my son, Marcos. With the money I was able to put him through higher education. He has gone on to be a bank executive, and that is thanks to the support of Fundacion Solidaridad.

'When I needed extra money, I came to Fundacion Solidaridad and they gave me some extra work, as well as the orders through the workshop. I was extremely grateful for that extra work which helped me to meet the expenses at home.

'After a few years, when my son had finished his education, I said I did not need this extra work any more, so hopefully someone else in need would be able to benefit from extra orders. The best thing is that we can work from home where we can keep an eye on our children.

'The importance of Fundacion Solidaridad is not just to do with the income. I live in a rural town and I have not only learned how to work, I also have developed my own personality.

'Before, my life was housework, take the kids to school and come back. Fundacion Solidaridad gave me a chance to grow as a person, to meet other people. Now I can do many different things. I know more about women's rights. I know how to manage my workload and also my money. I have learned how to argue with people, to express my point of view! I have learned a different reality.'

For Those Who Make the Arpilleras

In the unseasonal rain
I dream of you women,
your invisible hands
steering this long thin ship,*
the glide of your scissors and needles,
this gentle re-telling of history
with no movement of your faces,
the way you say
we at the soup kitchen could not speak out.
We turned skirts and blouses into pictures
that told of our frustrations.
These became our voices.

In this unseasonal rain
I dream of you, Margarita,
who sewed to put your children
through higher education
and Adriana, making lunch for your sick
   neighbour.
I hear your strong voices
drumming on Santiago's rooftops,
because of this
we have learned a different reality.

* Pablo Neruda described his homeland as a long thin ship.

Fiona Ritchie Walker
England

4

Springs of Hope

Advent Affirmations

Voice 1: We meet to worship God, to prepare the way of the Lord ...

Voice 2: People who live in fear ... they shall find new strength ...

Voice 3: so let us praise our God.

Voice 1: People who have lost their voice ... they shall sing for joy ...

Voice 2: so let us praise our God.

Voice 3: People who stumble ... they will jump and jive together ...

Voice 1: so let us praise our God.

Voice 2: People who are ignored ... they will be welcomed on the journey ...

Voice 3: so let us praise our God.

Voice 1: People who are bowed down with burdens ... they shall rise up like eagles ...

Voice 2: so let us praise our God.

Voice 3: This is what the prophets say and what John the Baptist declares,

Voice 1: and this is what we declare:

Voice 2: and all people shall know it – the goodness of our God!

Voice 3: so let us give thanks and praise our God, for ever and ever.

Graham Adams
England

Advent Hope

God of our desire and longing,
we await your coming with eager expectation
and with joyful hope.
Strengthen our hearts and minds
with the beckoning light of your redeeming love
that we may earnestly work for the coming of your
    kingdom
and be ever ready to receive you in those we meet.
    Amen.

Annabel Shilson-Thomas/CAFOD
England

Waiting with Hope

Children,
    flies on their faces
Wait in darkness

Women,
    chopping granite,
Wait in darkness

Men,
    migrant workers
Wait in darkness

Lord of Life
They wait with hope
For release from their bondage of poverty

Lord of Life
We wait with hope
For release from our bondage to riches

Lord of Active Compassion
Inspire us through
> Aid and Relief workers
> Peace activists
> Health practitioners
> Educationalists
> People of all ages
>> who accept challenges
>> take risks
so that people who wait in hope
will be liberated from oppression.

Geoffrey Duncan
England

Great Joy!

Light the Advent candles
Decorate the Christmas tree
Get ready!

Join the carol singers
Prepare the mince pies
Get ready!

Carol the old
Sing the new
Get ready!

So much for us ...
So little for others ...
Get ready ... to ...

prepare Christmas meals
buy new warm clothes and
receive the homeless
Get ready!

Prepare hot meals,
think about appropriate hospitality and
receive the destitute asylum seeker
Get ready ... so ...

that the world will have hope
and people will be treated with respect
and know peace
Great Joy!

Geoffrey Duncan
England

Blessèd Are You

Blessèd are you, the poor, the weak in spirit,
Heaven is yours, is yours!
Comfort to those who mourn and are now in distress.
Blessèd are you! Blessèd are you!

Blessèd are you, the meek, the low, the humble,
Yours is the earth, the earth!
Be satisfied, to do what our God most requires.
Blessèd are you! Blessèd are you!

Blessèd are you, those who are merciful to all,
You'll have God's mercy, God's mercy!
And with a pureness in your heart, you will see God.
Blessèd are you! Blessèd are you!

Blessèd are you, the peacemakers who long for hope,
You are God's children, God's children.

126

If you face hate when you talk of God's kingdom.
Blesséd are you! Blesséd are you!

Tune: Our God Reigns

Melanie Frew
England

Beatitudes – Upside-Down World

It seems a crazy way of looking,
like distorting mirrors at a fair,
to see mourners now are laughing,
to see hope where we see despair;
to see little people staring
in the world of kingdom come,
to see beggars now are wealthy
and our singers were the dumb.

But the eyes which see this vision
see the truth behind the face,
the word behind the headlines
which is spirit, hope and grace.
For the values of the kingdom
reverse what crowds now see,
and those values stand for ever,
they bless life eternally.

Bernard Thorogood
Australia

A Paraphrase of the Beatitudes

How liberated are those who have learnt to let go –
They shall experience the mystery of God.

How strong are those who are not afraid to admit their
weaknesses –
Their tears shall heal their grief.

How beautiful are those who reverence life –
The Earth shall rejoice in their presence.

How satisfied are those who long to serve God –
For God shall be their delight.

How happy are those who are willing to forgive others –
They shall find release from guilt and fear.

How enlightened are those who know oneness with all
    things –
They shall see God everywhere.

How inspiring are those who work for justice and peace –
They shall live as children of God.

What an opportunity there is for those who suffer in the
    cause of right –
Their rejection can become a doorway to new life.

W. L. Wallace
Aotearoa New Zealand

Beatitudes for Those Who Work with Disabled People

BLESSED ARE YOU who take time to listen to difficult
    speech
FOR YOU help us know that if we persevere, we can be
    understood.
BLESSED ARE YOU who walk with us in public places and
    ignore the stares of strangers,
FOR in your companionship, we find havens of relaxation.
BLESSED ARE YOU who never bid us to 'hurry up' and
    more blessed, you who do not snatch our tasks from our
    hands to do them for us
FOR often we need time rather than help.

BLESSED ARE YOU who stand beside us as we enter new
and untried ventures
FOR our failures will be outweighed by the time we
surprise ourselves and you.
BLESSED ARE YOU who ask for our help
FOR our greatest need is to be needed.
BLESSED ARE YOU who help us with the graciousness of
Christ
FOR often we need the help we cannot ask for.
BLESSED ARE YOU when, by all these things you assure
us that the thing that makes us individuals is not our
peculiar muscles, not in our wounded nervous systems,
nor in our difficulties in learning
BUT in the God-given self which no infirmity can confine.
REJOICE AND BE EXCEEDINGLY GLAD, and know that
you give us reassurances that could never be spoken in
words.
FOR you deal with us as Christ dealt with all his children.

Author Unknown

My Creed – My Beatitude

I believe in the precious nature of each individual.
Peace be to the people who respect their challenging and
exciting neighbours.

I believe in Justice for all people.
Peace be to the people who promote just and equal
opportunities for
humankind.

I believe in Human Rights for everyone.
Peace be to the people who support the right for
people to be
accepted for who they are.

I believe in the acceptance of women and men of whatever
sexual orientation and persuasion.
Peace be to the people who speak out against persecution,
bullying,
verbal and physical abuse of individuals and groups
of people.

I believe in an Inclusive Church.
Peace to the people who, with their love and desire for the
wholeness
of humankind, create communities and churches
where we are
enabled to worship in the spirit of diversity, honesty
and love.

Geoffrey Duncan
England

The Beatitudes: We Remember

We remember the poor; those who struggle to feed hungry
mouths and clothe malnourished bodies, who strive to
make homes from discarded waste and build a future from
shattered dreams. Lord, free us from our comfort, that with
them we may work towards the coming of God's kingdom.

Blessed are the poor
The kingdom of heaven is theirs.

We remember those who mourn; those whose hearts ache
and whose memories torment, who grieve for parent, sister,
partner, child, and who cry for themselves, for the lives they
once knew and have now lost. Lord, free our tears that we
may weep with them.

Blessed are those who mourn.
They shall be comforted.

We remember the meek; those who listen with intent and not with mild indifference, who persevere quietly where others make a noise, who brave the intolerable and seek to understand the different. Lord, free us from our fears that we may let go of our prejudices.

Blessed are the meek.
They shall inherit the earth.

We remember those who hunger and thirst for righteousness; those who long for justice and fight in the face of despair, who are fired by anger and compassion to pursue a vision and create a future. Lord, free us from our passivity, that we may join their struggle.

Blessed are those who hunger and thirst for righteousness.
They shall be satisfied.

We remember the merciful; those who are wronged but seek not revenge, who are hurt but seek to understand the pain, who refuse to be crippled by self-pity, but grapple with confusion so that bridges can be built. Lord, free us from a desire to forget, that we may learn to forgive.

Blessed are the merciful.
They shall have mercy shown to them.

We remember the pure in heart; those who seek to listen rather than to condemn, who refuse to blindly obey codes or live by rules, but who struggle to understand what is difficult and have the strength and courage to change. Lord, free us from self-righteousness, that we may embrace the fullness of life.

Blessed are the pure in heart.
They shall see God.

We remember the peacemakers; those who work for peace in the face of war, who strive for solutions in the wake of conflict, who refuse to be daunted by the abuse of power, and build bridges in places where others dare not tread. Lord, free us from apathy, that we may actively pursue all that leads to peace.

Blessed are the peacemakers.
They shall be called children of God.

We remember those who are persecuted, those who have the courage to challenge and to speak the truth, who are driven by the desire for justice and are moved by a spirit of compassion. Lord, free us from our sterility, that we may be emboldened to love.

Blessed are those who are persecuted for righteousness' sake.
The kingdom of heaven is theirs.

Annabel Shilson-Thomas
England

Coming for Many

In coming as a man,
Christ sanctified both sexes.
In holding little children,
Christ freed adults into play.
In speaking to women,
Christ unblocked the ears of all creation.
In touching the leper,
Christ blessed everyone,
no matter how unworthy they felt,
and opened a holy artery,
from heart to heart,
and hand to hand.
Praise God.

Duncan L. Tuck
England

Reach Out to Our Humanity

Compassionate God,
as your outstretched hands held a crucified world,
so let our hands convey the touch of love.
As you embraced our vulnerability
so cradle our hopes and fears.
Reach out to our humanity,
release our pain
and in your tenderness, bring healing to our brokenness
that in our weakness, we may find strength
and in our poverty, the unfurled riches of your
    resurrection.
Amen.

Annabel Shilson-Thomas/CAFOD
England

Morning Prayer

At the starting line of this day,
We call on your name, God of grace.
As we run the race you have set before us,
help us to keep our eyes on your goals, not our own.
When we falter, give us fresh strength and courage.
When we are fleet-footed, let us give you the glory.
Keep us from wanting to win at others' expense
or to count ourselves better than those at our side.
All runners are your children.
In the race you imagine,
each one is a winner.
Amen.

Carol Penner
Canada

133

God of Love and Love Abundant

God of Love and Love Abundant,
we give thanks for all your care.
You are making hate redundant
You give love enough to share.

Love of Life and Life Abundant,
born with grace to be mature.
God is making death redundant
God gives life that can endure.

Life of Hope and Hope Abundant,
boundless probability.
God is making fear redundant
God gives hope that sets all free.

Peace of God and God abounding,
guaranteeing every good.
Every evil now confounding
With intended family-hood.

Tune: St Catherine

David J. Harding
England

Hope for the World: Baptism in a Multi-racial Family of Faith

This baptism liturgy has been in use in a multi-racial church in the United States, a church where children of every skin colour play and pray together. It is a stunning sight to see a rainbow of children gather at the front to participate in the rite for a new entrant into the community. The baptism takes place immediately after the Children's Moment, so that the children can remain in the front of the church and participate in the liturgy.

Minister

Every child born into the world is a new thought from the mind of God, a fresh and radiant possibility. The sacrament of Baptism is a covenant between God and this family of faith in which we receive and bless this child _____ into the care and nurture of Christ's church, that the fresh and radiant possibilities in her/his tiny body may become manifest in her/his life. Baptism is an outward and visible sign of the grace of God, a sign and seal of our participation in God's forgiveness, and the beginning of growth into full Christian faith and discipleship.

Invitation to the parents, godparents and child to be baptised to come forward and gather around the font. The child's siblings, if she/he has any, should already be gathered with the other children in the centre front, and may come and stand with their parents.

Questions to the Parents

_____, do you, in bringing your child to be baptised, confess your faith in God, creator of all life and source of all love? If so, please say *I do*.

Do you recognise her/him as a child of God, created with her/his own individual worth and value, and do you promise to love her/him as an affirmation of that worth? If so, please say *I do*.

When you look at your child, will you see in her/him all the children of the world, of all races and nations, and know God's love for all humanity? If so, please say *I do*.

Will you share the joy and the power of the community of faith with her/him, and support her/his efforts to grow in Christian faith and discipleship? If so, please say *I do*.

Questions to the Godparents

_____, are you ready, with God's help, to guide and encourage _____, by counsel and example, in prayer and with love, to follow in the way of Jesus Christ? If so, please say *I am, with the help of God.*

Questions to the Children of the Community

Will you welcome _____ into our church family? If so, please say *I will.*

Will you play with her/him, and share your toys with her/him? If so, please say *I will.*

Will you teach her/him everything you know about Jesus, and help her/him to learn to sing and to pray and to praise God? If so, please say *I will, with the help of God.*

Will you comfort her/him when she/he is sad, invite her/him to play when she/he is lonely, and laugh with her/him when she/he is happy? If so, please say *I will, with the help of God.*

The acolyte, a child or youth, brings forward a pitcher of water. The minister prays as she pours the water into the font:

Loving God, we give you thanks for the gift of this child among us, and for the gift of your love which cleanses and refreshes us. Bless by your spirit this water. And by it, bless _____ this day, that she/he may live aware of your grace all the days of her/his life. Amen.

Act of Baptism

Prayer for the Baptised

Gracious God, you have filled the world with joy by giving

us the gift of Jesus as an infant, and by giving us this child, this new thought fresh from you. We know that _____ is your child. Give her/him strength for life's journey, courage in the time of suffering, the joy of faith, the freedom of love, and the hope of new life. Bless also _____ (her/his parents) and all the members of her/his extended family. May they always show their gratitude for the life you have given them by loving and caring for this little one. We pray all this through Jesus Christ, the lover of our souls. Amen.

The congregation is invited to speak their promises:
_____, we welcome you into the love and care of the Christian community. We promise to support and encourage your family in the fulfilment of their promises, and to stand with you in all the sorrows and joys of life, led by the way of Jesus, upheld by the love of God.

The Minister proceeds through the congregation with the child/infant in arms, trailed by the children of the congregation, while the congregation sings an appropriate hymn.

(Suggest: 'Child of Blessing, Child of Promise', *The New Century Hymnal*)

The Minister returns to the front with all the children in tow, and holds the baptised up for all to see, proclaiming:
Miracle of miracles! That so great a God lives in so frail a dwelling. Let us nurture the presence of God in this and every child.

The child is returned to the parents, who are given the baptismal certificate and gifts (including a candle made by children from the church). The rite is ended. All return to their seats.

Carla A. Grosch-Miller
England/USA

I Am the Light of the World

O Holy One, we have lost your way
  in a darkness of our own making.

We are in danger of
  foundering on our maximized profits;
  being swallowed up by our dog-eat-dog;
  drowning in our God-is-with-ME.
But you – in the self-giving love
  made down-to-earth and human
  in Jesus of Nazareth –
  are the Light of the World;
A beacon in our darkness
  warning us away
  from the shoals and shallows
  of our present course,
Pointing us to your deeper way –
  away from our I-know-who-God-is to your
  Such-knowledge-is-too-cosmic-for-me;
  from our Beware-the-enemy to your
  Be-aware-of-the-enemy-within.
Your Light of the World signals us
  that we, too, can be
  your light in our world.

Norm S. D. Esdon
Canada

Feeding 5,000 or More

Give thanks to God who gives us bread
and calls us still to share it out.
When faced with crowds who must be fed
'Thank God for gifts!' we sing and shout!

Give thanks to God for what seems small –
the humble things we bring and share;

138

With even these we can stand tall
for Christ sees in them how we care.

Give thanks to God who takes our bread
and helps us value others too;
that with these gifts the crowds are fed –
so may we work to see it through.

For thanks to God it can come true
if no one's gifts will be denied;
for with these gifts that start a few
all shall be fed and satisfied!

Graham Adams
England

I Am the Bread of Life

O Holy One, we measure each other
– and ourselves – by
   the bread we make
   the bread we have
   the bread we think we are;
But our bread is not your Bread.
Yours is the leaven in ours –
   your bread-and-wine
   in our meat-and-potatoes;
   your five-and-two-is-more-than-enough
   in our five-thousand-is-too-many;
   your now-is-the-time
   in our no-time-now;
   your above-board-discussion
   in our under-the-carpet-dissension;
   your raising-others-up
   in our putting-others-down;
   your highway in our desert,
     beacon in our darkness,

living vine in our dying garden,
doorway in our walls.
Bless you, Holy One, for being
your Healing Bread
in our ailing world.

Norm S. D. Esdon
Canada

Fruit of the Spirit

Voice One: Those born of the Spirit
are blessed with her fruit

Voice Two: They belong to a community of love
and express abundant joy.
They are the people of peace.

Voice One: Those born of the Spirit
are blessed with her fruit.

Voice Two: They know the virtue of patience in adversity;
towards needy neighbours, they show
kindness;
their lives are marked out by goodness.

Voice One: Those born of the Spirit
are blessed with her fruit.

Voice Two: In testing times, they walk by faith;
faced with anger, they respond with
gentleness;
attacked by extremists, they show self-control.

Voice One: Those born of the Spirit
are abundantly blessed with her fruit.

John Johansen-Berg
England

Gentle Spirit, Now Embracing

Gentle Spirit, now embracing
Men and women of each race,
From the plenum of the nations
Felt within all time and space.
Gather now in re-enactment,
Rushing wind and dipping flame,
May we speak in tongues of gladness,
Sing the glory of God's name.

With the coming of the Spirit,
With the faithful gathered round,
Hear them speaking of God's power,
See the gifts of grace abound.
Many witnessed with amazement,
Many plainly were perplexed,
Face to face with Holy Spirit,
In this world but of the next.

From amidst the loud confusion,
Simon Peter dared to speak:
'Soon the day will be upon us,
All flesh will God's Spirit seek.
Sons and daughters shall see visions
And the old shall dream new dreams.
Once more shall I pour my Spirit,
Leaving nothing as it seems.'

With the promise of salvation,
With the words of prophecy;
Came a wellspring for the future,
Lasting hope for all to see.
Moving down throughout the ages,
Still we find it in this place,

Moving outward from our worship,
Sharing with all gifts of grace.

Tune: Ode to Joy

Michael Jacob Kooiman
Canada

Roots Shoots and Fruits

Lord God,
Creator of the Tree of Life

We pray for roots,
Trying to provide foundation and security
in barren or hostile ground
Where it is difficult to root
or where strong winds blow
forcing them to hold on for the sake of the tree

We pray for those whose love and work is unseen
Holding things together
Providing nutrition and support
For individuals, families, churches

We pray for shoots
Signs of growth
Outlets for energy to burst forth
Tissues and leaves providing energy and growth
Shelter, shade
And a framework for fruits to be borne

We pray for those whose love and work is clearly seen
Seeking peace in times of conflict
Offering costly love, and even their lives
Love in action

We pray for fruits
Borne on shoots
Those who offer sustenance
To the hungry, the thirsty, and all in need
And those who through seeds
Can continue the cycle
Of planting, growth, seedtime and harvest

We pray for those whose love and work
Offers nourishment
Or a foundation for the future
Nourishing individuals and communities
Or planting new ventures
For others to develop and build

We pray for your church
It too is part of your cycle of renewal

You plant your people in fertile and rocky ground
Along the roadside as well as in fertile fields
Bless those who are roots, shoots or fruits
Strengthen and encourage them
Help them to understand their role in the kingdom
Seen or unseen
Part of your tree of life

In the name of Jesus Christ
Sower, vine dresser, leader of the harvest
Son of the Creator
Amen

Nick Butler
England

Here Is the News

Newsreaders finish – they go on their way,
And that is the end of the news for today:
but here is the news – God's Spirit is living
wherever there's helping and loving and giving.

There in our illness through love's tender care
Where comfort is given and sorrow is shared.

There in the darkness where some cannot cope,
in listening, restoring and giving new hope.

There in the famine where people are fed,
In help that is given to banish their dread.

There at the meetings where nations can build
a world made of friendship where all will be filled:
Yes, here is the News – God's Spirit is living
wherever there's helping and loving and giving.

Cecily Taylor
England

How Can We Stand, Ignoring Each Injustice?

How can we stand, ignoring each injustice?
How can we watch in silence, never learn
that making peace will bring the need to suffer,
absorbing hatred on the cross of love?

Here is the challenge facing every Christian:
to raise again the cross on which Christ died;
no metaphor, no easy resurrection,
our cup, like his, is not an easy draught.

So can we die, yes, offer no resistance,
save that of love, our lives poured out as grace;

144

to freely proffer hope where life is desperate
to raise the dying, comfort those who hate?

Tune: Metre 11.10.11.10

Andrew Pratt
England

Seeing Christ's Face in Haiti

Moving in and out of excess and starkness, wealth and
    poverty.
Shock. Awe. Exhaustion.
The stench of open sewers; the aroma of bougainvilleas.
Ice kept cool by sawdust; refrigerated ice clinking in
    glasses.
Children crawling over mounds of garbage seeking
    treasure; new shoes and new ruffles in church.
Corrugated iron walls ready to collapse in the next wind;
    gingerbread trim above cool terraces and wicker chairs.
An old battered plastic doll; high-tech video equipment.
Anger; peace.
Rage; in the everlasting arms.
Shame; the peace of Christ be with you.
Guilt; shalom.
How do I reconcile my wealth with your poverty?
My power with your powerlessness?
My freedom with your captivity?
My choices with your survival existence?
My education with your inability to go to school?
My wheels with your calloused feet?
My lunch with your hunger?
My all with your nothing?

God, forgive us for we know not what we do. Forgive us, for
when we see your children naked, we remain blind. Forgive
us, for when we hear the blood of our sister or brother crying

from the ground, we remain deaf. Forgive us when we smell sour humanity and call it roses.

We worship on the edge of the City de'Soleil where four million people live compacted in an area one mile by four miles in size. Where hope of a future turns into the despair of today. We praise God in an upper room church. We are welcomed. We receive blessings. We dance while the drums, electric guitars and keyboard belt out a Bob Marley tune after worship.

We drive through City de'Soleil with locked doors and closed windows. The heat of the day beats through the van's metal sides. We drink water from our sterilized water bottles knowing the sewer water running alongside the street is all that many outside the van will ever taste.

We rejoice at the bronze image of a young tall black man reaching for a dove, standing above the intertwined bodies of those who died in the coup. We marvel at the bronze image of the man who liberated Haiti in 1804 to make it the first Black nation in the 'Western World'. We celebrate with the bronze image of the young soul called 'liberty' pulling away from leg chains.

Surely we have seen Christ's face a thousand times today.

Ana K. Gobledale
Australia/USA

5

Hope for Today's World

I Dream of a Church

I dream of a church that joins in with God's laughing
as she rocks in her rapture, enjoying her art
she's glad of her world, in its risking and growing:
'tis the child she has borne and holds close to her heart.

I dream of a church that joins in with God's weeping
as she crouches, weighed down by the sorrow she sees:
as she cries for the hostile, the cold and no-hoping –
for she bears in herself our despair and dis-ease.

I dream of a church that joins in with God's dancing
as she moves like the wind and the wave and the fire:
a church that can pick up its skirts, pirouetting,
with steps that can signal God's deepest desire.

I dream of a church that joins in with God's loving
as she bends to embrace the unlovely and lost:
a church that can free, by its sharing and daring,
the imprisoned and poor – and then shoulder the cost.

God, make us a church that joins in with your living,
as you cherish and challenge, reign in and release,
a church that is winsome, impassioned, inspiring:
lioness of your justice and lamb of your peace.

Kate Compston
England

We Dream of a Church

We dream of a church that will live as a movement,
set free from the boundaries and walls we create,
and move towards Jesus who moves beyond borders
to liberate people who dream as they wait.

We dream of a church that will live out its story,
proclaiming new life for earth's people this day;
a church that re-learns its traditions of justice
by sharing as equals and friends on the way.

We dream of a church that will nurture potential,
identify prejudice, conflict and fear,
and strive for a world where we all work as partners
by building God's future-koinonia right here.

We dream of a church that will risk reputation,
compassion exceeding obsessions with gain;
courageous in face of complacent resistance
by caring for neighbours and outcasts the same.

We dream of a church that will join with God's passion:
may earth be restored and its peoples at peace!
We trust as we journey without all the answers
that God's love will guide us and hope shall not cease.

Graham Adams
England

The Flower

God look into my eyes
as a child looks at a flower.

You are beautiful and small.
You are tenderly made fragile.
Your colours delight and confuse.

148

And so God touches me gently.
For though I am weak, small and confusing,
God's world would be less colourful without me.

Ed Cox
England

Through the Eyes of the Young

Youthful King,
as you anointed David, as a young man,
to reign over all Israel,
we give you thanks
for trusting a nation to the vision of a youth.

**Help us to see your kingdom through the eyes of the
young.**

As you called Samuel, as a boy,
to speak your words of prophesy,
we ask for your openness,
that we might listen to the words of children.

**Help us to see your kingdom through the eyes of the
young.**

As Mary sat at the feet of Jesus,
eager to learn of your life and your love,
teach us to worship you
with the devotion and imagination of children.

**Help us to see your kingdom through the eyes of the
young.**

As Jesus, son of Mary,
shocked the leaders of the synagogue with his youthful
wisdom,

challenge us
to seek out the young prophets in our congregation.

**Help us to see your kingdom through the eyes of the
young.**

Ed Cox
England

Note from God

When they cut the cord
and branded you bastard,
I was there.

When your father left,
when your mother wept,
I was there.

When she turned
to her brother for comfort,
I was there.

I was in
your mother's arms
your uncle's eyes –

I was the porch light,
the place at table,
the bed where they laid you,

I took you in,
I was there.

Denise Bennett
England

Special Offer

One new day –
not two for the price of one;
one new day.

The sea has washed clean
of all footprints
yesterday's beach.

Go well into
this new day –
an unrepeatable bargain!

Cecily Taylor
England

I Am the Doorway

O Holy One, we build walls
you open doorways through them.
When we wall others out (walling ourselves in)
you open us to the other side:
    When pride walls us in
    you open us to reconciliation;
    When fear-of-rejection walls us in
    you open us to self-acceptance;
    When Keep-out-the-strange! walls us in
    you open us to Entertain-angels-unaware;
    When Are-we-there-yet? walls us in
    you open us to Have-we-seen-here-yet?
    When That's-not-fair! walls us in
    you open us to see – nailed to a cross –
    your down-to-earth human
    doorway between
        earth and heaven
        death and life
        this and the other side.

O Holy One, in our world of walls
guide us to the doorway to
your more open world.

Norm S. D. Esdon
Canada

Think of a World that Could Be ...

Think of a world that could be;
too long have greed and hatred raged,
by our own hand the world is caged,
how can the kingdom come?
Is harmony an idle dream,
justice and mercy but a scheme
only reserved for some?

Pray for a world that can be,
when self is routed from its lair
and love becomes the rightful heir –
pray that this time will be:
when, all the earth is loved and shared,
ravaged, polluted things repaired,
all creatures join the plea.

Work of a world that must be:
it's not enough to sit and hope,
or dimly wish and blindly grope –
the dawn can speed the night.
The time is now – before too late,
before we are destroyed by hate –
for love needs lamps to light.

Sing of a world that shall be;
its rays of hope break through the gloom,
and now awaking from our tomb
we walk to meet the sun:
transmuting wrong, as love has taught,

the Spirit's alchemy is wrought –
the will of God is done.

Cecily Taylor
England

A Prayer for Openness

Jesus, you open us
to new life, new hope, new possibilities.
You conquer the way we
close up, close down, and close in.

Jesus, lover of us all,
open our hearts to feel your compassion
for people we would rather walk by;
open our ears to hear the cries of the suffering
deep inside where we cannot fail to be moved;
open our understanding to new ways of living
that do not diminish anyone;
open our eyes to see a vision of this world
as you would have it.

May these prayerful words on our lips
become the meditations of our hearts
as we live in ways that are acceptable to you
O God, our Rock and our Redeemer.
Amen.

Carol Penner
Canada

Dreamer at Prayer

God of creation, Designer supreme,
Our sensitive weaver of action or dream
With praise we adore you, we feast on your gaze,
Endearing, unending, O radiance of days.

God of the landscape, dear God of all life,
May you, our provider, forgive us for strife,
For those who face drought and daily distress
May your spirit guide us, the needy to bless.

To God of the workplace, to God of all skills,
We bring you our thanksgiving, we offer our wills,
With you and your colleagues let's work with our hands
To love and to cherish; to pray for all lands.

God of the flat-share, the commune and home,
We pray for the rootless, wherever they roam,
Whatever their story, whatever our song,
Lord, bring us together, that all may belong.

God of all unions, all parties, all creeds,
Bring us to new life through being, not deeds
In the name of the Parent, the Spirit, the Son
As God's healing leads us, may all become one.

God of the Cosmos, great God beyond time,
When restrictions beset us, or sorrow or crime,
Be close to support us, ordain us as thine
Through grace and through wholeness may forgiving light
    shine.

God of all certainty, God of all trust,
Please take our confusions and turn them to dust,
Relieve us of stresses, your hope to reveal
As seeds of renewal we discover will heal.

Source of humanity, help us to see
The vision of peace is ours to foresee,
Remake us and mould us, your dreams to review
Let your vision guide us true faith to pursue.

Wendy Whitehead
England

A Resting Place

Hope is
a resting place
beside
life's climbing way
where
we can pause
to check
our trusted maps.
We may not stay;
still less expect
such sure support
when we forget
to pray
with those
like us confined
by what
the best guides
say.

David J. Harding
England

Future Tense and Present Tense

It will all come right in God's good time –
so the proper preachers say –
just wait, be patient, bear with it now
and you will see a glorious way.

That's not the way we think today.
Salvation's always up ahead
somewhere still to come, some hope
in worlds to come when we are dead.

We need our hoping grounded here
where longing, striving fuel our race,

and not in some far paradise
beyond our sight, our time, our space.

Today, to hear the children laugh
and no more beggars on the street,
today to find the law is just
and tyrants toppled from their seat.

Today are broken victims freed
and blind eyes catch the morning light;
today we shout God's jubilee;
today the text is proven right.

A foretaste now, a gleam of light,
to challenge every voice of doom,
that is the presence of the Lord
who stands, in light, beyond the tomb.

Bernard Thorogood
Australia

We Stayed for Coffee*

We stayed for coffee and biscuits.
We shared conversation together and
caught a glimpse of the
Love of Marginalised People.

They shared stories of their lives.
We listened to each other and
learned anew of the
Compassion of the Dispossessed.

They presented us with a challenge.
We talked about ways of living together and
came near to the reconciling
Spirit of Justice, Joy and Peace.

**Let us celebrate and
share love, compassion and justice.**

*In rural and remote parts of south India it is a wonderful tradition of
hospitality that, whatever their circumstances families always serve coffee or
tea and biscuits.*

Geoffrey Duncan
England/south India

An Optimistic View

(No poverty in the twenty-second century, only in the poverty museum?)

There is a strong feeling among youth and a great sense of
responsibility from the rich countries, to end world poverty
through fair trade, debt cancellation and better aid. I strong-
ly feel that we can create a poverty-free world. As we know,
each and everyone is unique with inbuilt qualities and
everyone has potential and imagination. The basic ingredi-
ent to overcome poverty is packed inside each poor person
like a battery. All we need to do is create opportunities to
help the person unleash this energy and creativity. Once this
is done, poverty will disappear very fast.

I believe the only place in the world where poverty may
exist will be in the poverty museums, no longer in human
society.

Anil K. Patil
South India/England

A Reflection from Haiti

'As a mother comforts her child, so will I comfort you' Isaiah 66.13

The mother sits almost swallowed in the shadows. Her
bright patterned skirt contrasts with her dull and sunken
skin. Her thin arms encircle her child, suckling at her breast.
Homeless? Hungry? Close to despair? I wonder as we
rumble past on our bus touring Haiti. The image left in my

mind is how hopeless she appears, yet she has strength and love enough to continue providing nourishment for her infant. Persisting with hope.

So God sticks with us, comforting us when all is bleak. When God looks at the world, as Jesus looked at Jerusalem, and weeps, God's love never shuts off. When God's creation is ravaged through deforestation and mining, God never fails to give us hope. When God's people are crammed into stricken sewage-infested areas, God persists to nourish and offer hope. When souls and bones are broken by racism, economic and political greed, God's compassion re-lights the flame of hope.

God comforts those who rest in God's embrace. God nourishes those who draw on God's power. God invites us to be comforted and nourished, like helpless infants. God invites us to receive divine nourishment and grow in stature and faith. God invites us to receive the power to re-light the flame of hope in our world, and to nourish the weakest and poorest of God's children.

As a mother comforts her child, so God comforts us.
As a mother comforts her child, so are we called to comfort others.

**God, hold us in your embrace and comfort us in our pain.
Nourish us with your love and grace.
Light in us the flame of hope that we might carry it to every corner of your creation.
Amen.**

*Ana K. Gobledale
Australia/USA*

A Litany of Hope

Leader: It is unacceptable
that some should starve
whilst others eat too much.

**Response: Let us share the bread of life,
that people may be given hope.**

Leader: It is unacceptable
that some should lack a home
whilst houses stand empty.

**Response: Let us build homes,
that all may have a shelter.**

Leader: It is unacceptable
that some should live in poverty
whilst billions are spent on weapons.

**Response: Let us learn to trust each other,
that resources may be devoted to the needy.**

Leader: It is unacceptable
that children should die
for lack of clean water.

**Response: Let us learn to live simply,
that others may have the water of life.**

John Johansen-Berg
England

Tap Dancing

Fresh sparkling water flows through the garden turning all
to lush, green pasture ...
precious water, life-giving, free-to-all water ...

A tap is turned.

The flow is stopped and the hand that turns the power
reversing the garden to a barren desert.
Creation becomes uncreation
Water and food withdrawn at once.

The dancing children stall and turn,
their eyes of laughter sink into their cheeks,
fit to burst,
begging for life.

Water, flowing and pure, against water, stagnant and
    diseased.
So easily, at a turn of a tap.
Life is death, unhappy neighbours, sit side by side.
How is this justice?
… Those who have …
… Those who have not …
The spring of life is extinguished with the turn of a tap.

Tap, tap, tap.

And the political dance goes on.

The turn of a tap

And life can flow again. Justice at last, essentials for all.
    So easy, so easy.

We are the brothers and sisters of our world,
sitting side by side,
children who may dance in the rainbow of water and light.
Hope for the world.

Martin Hazell
England

Celebrating Christmas

Incredible when you think of it
The source of all our merriment
An upstart of the labour class
Who in searching anguish came to pass.
More astounding when it be known
His plans to reign and the rich dethrone.

Risky business, this celebration
When every day's a Christmas Season.
Legal rights, education,
Help these least find just one reason
To be human, to hear their call
To take their place among the tall.

Lift up the lowly? Not a chance.
There's more to life. Can't spare a glance.
Besides, I need them. Don't we all?
Who else would be at our beck and call?

How will we respond, I wonder,
As God's mighty hand tears us asunder;
Servants gone, only workers;
Class and caste in the past;
No keeping up or looking down
Only *Emmanuel* – God with us.

Deep within the jingle, jingle,
Bells do toll – feel a tingle?
Blood to shed as bread we break
There's a cause to celebrate.

Astrid Lobo Gajiwala
India

161

Hoping and Longing for Change and Release

(Palm Sunday)

Hoping and longing for change and release
Looking for someone to make their pain cease
People are running to join with the crowd
Waving their branches, their shouting grows loud

Man on a donkey, can you lead the way
Out of this darkness into a new day?
Will you defeat those who rule us by sword?
Lead us to victory – be our strong Lord

Is this the one who will set us all free?
Has the time come to expect victory?
Hopeful the questions directing their feet,
Longing to see their oppressors retreat

Soon they must learn that such dreams come to nought
His not the triumph that they would have sought
Love, only love guides the path he will take
Love that, through dying, to new life will break

Longing and hoping in lands far and near
Voices of suffering people we hear
Calling for justice, for healing, for peace
Still they need someone to make their pain cease

Let us then open our hearts as did he
Friends of that man on a donkey, may we
Faced with the agony of this world's pain
Learn from his love how to bring life again

Tune: Trisagion

Wendy Ross-Barker
England

From the Deep Recesses of Our Souls,
We Cry Out ...

Here we are: pastors, mentors, community workers,
   mothers,
     wives
       thrown into the dark abyss of oppression.
       Despair and loneliness churn within us
          for we are misunderstood,
             marginalised,
             minusculed
             by family, work, church and society.

The formidable walls of patriarchy hem us in,
          making drab and lifeless
          what once was colourful and throbbing

     BUT

Let not the pain immobilise us ...
Let not the fear destroy us ...
Let not the lashings drive us to our knees ...

For we have come together to unearth our hurts
That these may become,
To each one of us,
A source of strength and bonding.

We have come to name
That which maims us that,
By naming it, we might control and,
Perhaps,
Dispel it.

We have come to gingerly cradle in our bosoms
The truth and the power
That will free us to make us

     Women of Dignity:
     Women of Courage;
     Women of Love;

That we may stand and struggle
Alongside all those who cry
From the deep recesses of their souls.

Sharon Rose Joy Ruiz-Duremdes
Philippines

The Dough is Rising

The dough is rising
The frond unfurling
The people's hope is growing
For justice everywhere.

The flower is fruiting
The grape fermenting
The people's search is spreading
For spirit everywhere.

The leaves are falling
The winter coming
Come join the growing longing
For new life everywhere.

But Earth is crying
The creatures dying
Come save this threatened planet
From deadness everywhere.

When hearts are bonding
When prayer shapes doing
Then sacred ways of caring
Shall free life everywhere.

W. L. Wallace
Aotearoa New Zealand

Recognise the Joy

When we can see
just one bright light
once pierce the darkness
of a night,
or feel
a single stirring breeze
across an age of calm,
discern a hint of love
where love seems lost
or find a leaf
from some far distant tree
we recognise with joy
these signs
of reservoir,
oasis symbols
of unseen
resource
and have to celebrate
now and again
the goodness, gracious God
whose lively loving
stretches
in and out
and up and down
and round about
and far beyond
what we can see.

David J. Harding
England

In Celebration of Unconventional Friendships

Long before I heard her story
or knew the reason for her change of name,
our friendship had begun to grow.

It is rooted in the soil of shared interests,
deep conversations,
lighthearted playfulness,
delight in each other's company,
mischievous pleasure in trying to set the world to rights.

It does not delineate
who is the giver,
who the receiver.
It draws no false dichotomy
between need and support.
We value the freedom it offers
to be ourselves and to minister to each other,
outside the confines of labels or roles.

I thank God for this and other friendships
in my eclectic, extended family,
which cross the barriers and boundaries
of other people's narrower expectations.
The friendships of Jesus might be seen like this too.

Hope springs eternal,
bursts forth into flower
from such unconventional soils.
Give thanks for all to whom you relate in similar ways.

Jean Mortimer
England

Commitment to Hope

Loving God,
I bring my life to you.
Help me live as you would choose.

Creative God,
I present my gifts to you.
Help me work to bring beauty to the world.

Compassionate God,
I open my heart to you.
Help me feel the needs of others.

Ever-present God,
I entrust my soul to you.
Help me commit to justice and peace.

Healing God,
I give you my wounds.
Help me grow in your love.

Empowering God,
I seek your strength.
Help me strive to become like you.

Nurturing God,
I need your truth.
Help me live as one with hope.

Louise Margaret Granahan
Canada

On Earth as in Heaven

There is no heaven, so the young man said,
Life is an empty dream, we end up dead,
No angel choirs, no sound, no life, no light,
No God to guide us home through death's dark night.

But here where the blue-green sea reflects the sky,
Here where the white-winged seagulls love to fly,
Here where the castle's ruins o'erlook the shore,
The entrance to heaven becomes an open door.

Death as the final word is not God's plan,
The grave cannot destroy what God began
When from the dust our human form he made,
God lifts us to the light from death's dark shade.

The night approaches now the sun is low,
The shore reflects the sunset's golden glow.
Such beauty soothes the soul, it cannot die,
At one with the ebbing tide, the seagull's cry.

Heaven is where with God we find release
From gloom, despair, from all that mars our peace,
God in the storm, and God in the sunlit shore
Walking beside us, God who unlocks heaven's door.

John Stephenson
England

Our World

Our world is one world:
what touches one affects us all –
the seas that wash us round about,
the clouds that cover us,
the rains that fall.

Our world is one world:
the thoughts we think affect us all –
the way we build our attitudes,
with love or hate, we make
a bridge – or wall.

168

Our world is one world:
its ways of wealth affect us all –
the way we spend, the way we share,
who are rich or poor,
who stand or fall?

Our world is one world:
just like a ship that bears us all –
where fear and greed make many holes,
but where our hearts can hear
a different call.

Tune: Chernobyl

Cecily Taylor
England

I Am a Loveable, Creative Person

All: I am a loveable, creative person
made in the likeness of God.
I give myself permission to enjoy being myself
   to love without fear of rejection,
   to create with imagination,
   to change without dread of the future,
   to use my power responsibly,
   to work for justice and peace
   and live as a singer and dancer
   within God's all-embracing being.

W. L. Wallace
Aotearoa New Zealand

I Am the Way

O Holy One, we have portrayed our faith
   as 'The Only True Religion'
But our way is not your way:

You are self-giving love
   love that gives of itself –
   no self-serving attached;
You are this way
   made down-to-earth and human
   in Jesus of Nazareth;
You point the way
   not to, but through him
   to your down-to-earth way
   of salvation offered
   to every earth-dwelling human;
You call us to choose self-giving love
   in our self-serving world of
   traumatizing terror
   and twisted truth;
Through him you show the way
   and the truth and the life of
   self-giving love –
   our self-serving world's
   only salvation.

Norm S. D. Esdon
Canada

All Creation Hopes

Rising suns, guiding stars,
Fields and meadows awaiting rain,
Snowdrops, climbing ivy,
Blossoming apple trees,
Ripening grain,
Clusters of grapes,
Ancient trees laden with olives,
Acorns nestled in autumn leaves.

Birds building nests,
Lost lambs bleating,

Mating calls of moose,
Whales suckle their pups.

Fishermen casting their nets,
Indians harvesting plants,
Workmen waiting to be hired,
Racers stepping to the starting line.

A beggar stretching forth her hand,
A mother's prayer for her unborn child,
An intercessor at Lourdes,
A penitent at the altar.

The empty cross, the empty tomb,
The power of Pentecost,
Hope eternal.

Pearl Willemssen Hoffman
USA

In Our Silence

Finding our God-self in our silence
gives us the capacity to restore harmony,
lay healing upon old wounds,
still our restless mind,
cradle our own small griefs,
prepare ourselves for when life calls.
Then, we can reach out to those in need
and hold them in our prayers.

Eve Jackson
England

Thankful People Sing Their Praise to You

Bright morning maker, as your sun breaks through,
dawn's early light reflects in morning dew.
So thankful people sing their praise to you:
Alleluia

Daylight creator, through the busy day,
sun, chasing shadows, drives the clouds away
and in the rush of life we pause to say:
Alleluia

Lifetime companion, in the evening light,
sunset throws colours at the approaching night
and weary hearts are lifted by the sight:
Alleluia

Night-time's safe keeper, when we take our rest,
lift darkening fears from those who are distressed.
Grant us your peace and may our sleep be blessed:
Alleluia

Tune: Sine Nomine

Marjorie Dobson
England

After Ascension

Down to earth Jesus, in you God is known,
By your teaching and healing, his love you have shown,
By words that speak truth and by challenging wrong,
The powerless find hope and the weak are made strong.

Down to earth Jesus, now hidden from view,
Your voice is unheard and no hand can touch you,
And yet, through all those who still follow your way,
You live and reach out to the world of today.

172

Down to earth Jesus, who prayed for us then,
Come and join us with you and the Father again.
Lord, make us all one, then your truth we will show,
Till all the world's people towards unity grow.

Tune: Slane

Wendy Ross-Barker
England

God Is Known in Many Ways

(Trinity and Christian Aid)

God is known in many ways,
His great love invites our praise.
We will make our voices sound,
Spread his goodness all around.

All about us we can see
God at work in plant and tree ...
Food for life that all may share,
Given into human care.

Jesus teaches us to give
So that others too may live.
He has shown us how to care
For God's children everywhere.

Through his Spirit, out of sight,
God keeps working day and night ...
Using generous human hands
To bring hope across all lands.

By our gifts, our prayers, our deeds
We'll respond to human needs
Longing, working, till at last
Pain and poverty are past.

Tune: Ephraim

Wendy Ross-Barker
England

Hymn upon the Publication of a Church Cookbook

*(in the hope that all of the commandments therein be observed faithfully,
frequently and fruitfully)*

O for a thousand tongues to taste
This bounty of fine food.
May nothing here be dished in haste
Or serve to amplify the waist
And not our sense of good.

Praise fruits and spices, fresh or dried:
Maize, manna, cinnamon.
A banquet angels are denied
In flighty, disembodied stride,
But rained on women, men.

Sing we our Savior's savored blend
Con gusto, gratitude.
Our psalms in salmon, scaled, panned,
Our gospel in gazpacho, and
The bean's beatitude.

Be blest our home's aromas all,
Things zesty, crusty, chewed.
Smells waft like incense through the wall
And hold us in high oven's thrall
And stewy certitude.

In blender's whirr, in spoonly torque,
In all that's stir and grind.
In perk of kettle, cloop of cork,
In lurk of sizzle, soup, and fork,
We'll deep communion find.

To dine alone is not Thy wish,
'Tis seed that's vainly spilled.
God, multiply each meager dish

Till famine fades in loaf and fish,
And none may go unfilled.

Tune: Rest

Edward Moran
USA

Shedding Light

(Quaker Meeting)

From the silence,
a gift of words;

ministry
which reminds me –

after the storm
there will be calm,

after the darkness
there will be sunrise –

that it is in giving
I gain.

Denise Bennett
England

One Single Word

One single word
spoken at the right time
can make all the difference.

This is a good time.
Today I'm cloud-walking,

clear skies above,
head and shoulders above everything else,
treading on air
with cotton wool beneath my feet.

Life is good.

For once, I feel achievement
bolstering my confidence.
There is praise and respect
and people look at me
in a different light.

But it will not always be so.

Lord, keep me safe
when suddenly the clouds fall away,
when turbulence is inevitable,
when I must come down
from dizzy heights
and touch the earth again.

Grant me a safe landing
and the ability to keep going
and to maintain the faith
until it is time to take off again.

Marjorie Dobson
England

God Comes in Unexpected Ways

God comes in unexpected ways
to interrupt our fast:
the needy face, the unseen hand
bring love to grow and last.

Such faces go unrecognized.
The Christ we fail to see
is hidden in a shifting crowd
of lost humanity.

The words we speak are platitudes,
an empty, hollow creed
until we risk, hold out our hand,
and feel our neighbour's need.

Tune: Any common metre

Andrew Pratt
England

Hoping in God's Dream

The call to be Christian
is a call to hope in God's dream
here in Aotearoa New Zealand
the land of hopes, the land of dreams.

A thousand years or so ago, people came to this land
hoping for a new place in which to live and to dream.
This land of Aotearoa, this land of the Long White Cloud,
became home to people rich in culture and spirit.

Two hundred years ago, white men and women,
white adventurers and settlers came to this land,
to build a new life, to begin again,
to hope and to dream in a new way.

The hopes and dreams of these two peoples met in this
    land.
Hope of a shared dream, a treaty partnership,
flickered but would not come to be.

The European dream proved unwilling,
unable to hear the dream already present in this land.

Another hope, another dream, arose between the great
    wars.
A dream of community responsibility,
of affordable housing, of free education and of healthcare,
a dream of a social safety net for the most in need.

Yet for many, this too has been shattered.
Many in Aotearoa New Zealand still struggle
with unemployment, poverty, homelessness, and
    exclusion.
Many have lost hope and lost the ability to dream.

Today the driving force is not life-giving human dreams
but market legitimated greed and competition.
This ideology leaves no room
for different hopes or different dreams.

As people of faith we open ourselves
to the dream that resonates through Scripture.
The dream that began to be realised,
in and through the Exodus, the covenant and the Jubilee
    Laws.

The dream to which the prophets of old,
continually had to call the people back
The dream of Jesus' new heaven and a new earth,
that is genuinely Good News to the Poor.

God's hope today for us
is that we recover God's dream for Aotearoa New Zealand
that we enable others to hope and to dream
and that we give flesh to the Good News.

Together we can recover the Treaty relationship
and the commitment to social responsibility.
Together we can challenge the market thinking
and even hope for a just future for all the world.

David Tutty
Aotearoa New Zealand

Africa

I have heard about
Africa. A country full of corruption, fraud, poor
governance. Strip mining eroding the land, climate
change, the encroaching desert. HIV/AIDS killing a
generation, polio, malaria. Dirty water miles from home, dried
wells and privatisation at any cost. Aid not reaching the needy,
poorly planned, conditionality. Trade barriers imposed by the wealthy,
flooded markets, failed industry. I saw Africa. A joyous place full of
people committed to change, to help themselves.
A place that values education, loves life and
has hope. Homes taking in orphaned
children, loving the sick, praying
for the dying. A continent of
sun, laughter, song. 57
countries, all different, all
precious. 620,000,000 signs of
hope. Thank you for
showing me Africa.
Thank you for
Africa.

Melanie Frew
England

Rethinking Hope

Hope is not an emotion
it is a responsibility,
calling us to affirm
our work for justice
and trust in God's righteousness.

Hope is not a feeling
it is an action,
demanding our work
for those who suffer
and those who are oppressed.

Hope is not an idea
it is a promise,
challenging us
to be different
and accept the other.

Hope is not a belief
it is a pledge,
that we will challenge injustice
and welcome the stranger
even when we fear.

Hope is not a notion
it is a commitment,
to feed the child
to hold someone with AIDS
and see God in each face.

Hope is not a gift
it is a burden,
asking us to walk
in the way of Christ
and love with actions not words.

Louise Margaret Granahan
Canada

Remembering Hiroshima

Young people float candles on a lake.
Mothers wave placards in a town square.
Survivors paint their memories: a record of the lost,
shocking images relived in hope their suffering will stop.
People all over the world unite in prayer.

Eve Jackson
England

God Who Creates and then Colours the Earth

God who creates and then colours the earth,
paints it with beautiful features –
oceans and islands, and forests and beasts –
preparing for reasoning creatures.

Sinful or pure, doubtful or sure,
God comes to those who are ready or not;
woman or male, healthy or frail,
God wants us all to be part of the plot.

God who calls Adam and Noah and Abe,
Moses and monarchs and seers,
fashions a people he claims for his own –
how odd! – in the land of Judea.

God who sends angels to Mary and Joe,
earthing the dream of Isaiah,
guides surprised shepherds and wise men to go
and witness the birth of Messiah.

God who empowers the Christ in his work,
scribes and disciples amazing,
sends his own Son to his suffering and death,
but saves the whole world by his raising.

God who continues his mission through saints –
folk overwhelmed by his glory;
still he is here after zillions of years
and writing us into his story.

Tune: Here's to the Maiden

Kim Fabricius
Wales/USA

The Shape of Water

This morning, as clouds promise rain,
I see clearly the shape of water: huge drops
splashing on roads, in patterns as puddles,
acres awash, the rushing of rivers,
gushing from pipes, taps flowing,
in tanks full to overflowing,
boreholes and wells, reservoirs
and man-made lakes.

Please God, whatever it takes,
may the shape of things to come
be clean water for everyone.

Eve Jackson
England

The River of God

A Reflection

We came to the river of God thirsty and tired. Wondered why there were no fences to keep us out and we stood for a moment in the water up to our ankles. Noticing how slowly it flowed ... respecting our own freedom to move and to choose ... noticing how good the sand felt under our bare feet. How the sun warmed our skin.

Somehow we just knew the river contained only love ... flowing from the source of all creation ... flowing towards the future ... where anything that is not love is absorbed and dissolved.

And we walked deeper into the water up to our knees marvelling at how little pressure there was ... how we could change direction if we wanted ...

And we became aware that we wanted to go deeper and so we walked slowly forward until the water reached first our waist then our breasts and our shoulders ... Still we could see right to the bottom ... still we knew it was our choice, our freedom ... knew we could go back.

And then we reached the point where to go further we'd have to lift our toes off the sandy bottom and let the river of God carry us wherever it flowed ... some of us did step off in faith ... and some of us remained to enjoy the flow of the love around us ... But we were in it and we were changed ... when we surrendered to its peace, its compassion and its mercy.

Diane Gilliam-Weeks
Aotearoa New Zealand

The One Not There

The one not there is always turning up.
We can't help bowing to the empty chair
where, large as life, his honour sits to sup.

Those whose belief in him is one hiccup
find he is everywhere but where they stare
and, though not there, is always turning up.

The powers unseen don't need the guns of Krupp,
Pandora's not the only conjuror there.
The absent guest invites himself to sup.

183

Petitioners of air are sold a pup,
save for the trembling consequence of prayer,
the one not there who will keep turning up.

Forebear to fax him with your guff or gup:
he'll make his presence felt although elsewhere
and, as he said, is with us as we sup.

The one who doesn't come will fill the cup
of those who've loved until the cupboard's bare.
For one not there he will keep turning up
and, there or not, rubs shoulders as we sup.

Brian Louis Pearce
England

be-*Christ*-ing Church

Unknown so intimately, Christ
    you dare confront us with God's love:
a love that risks belief in us;
    a love encircling like a dove.

You shaped a movement changing lives:
    still now it moves to change again;
but see how, shaped by worldly fear,
    it longs to last but stay the same.

So Christ, unknown though learnt by heart,
    come to us, in this church of yours,
to breathe new life and build on hope
    embracing both our faith and flaws.

For this, your future which we seek,
    will only come about through change –
the kind of change you dared embrace:
    the force of grace that made you strange!

And yes, we dare to want that force:
  for as it made you strangely warm,
as boundless love possessed your life,
  it caused a brave new world to dawn.

So help us, Christ, to claim such nerve,
  that grace becomes our way to be,
resisting fearful common-sense,
  be-*Christ*-ing church with liberty!

Tune: O Waly, Waly

Graham Adams
England

Celebration of Hope

There are times when I feel despairing,
when all around seems dark
and my cry for help is unheard.
Then, unexpected, a faint light appears,
gradually dispersing the darkness.
The silence is broken
by the sound of angelic voices.
I know that God has heard my cry
and reaches out to heal me.
I experience transforming power.
Now, I know what changes can be made
by a community of love.

John Johansen-Berg
England

Who is Christ?

Who is Christ if not our teacher
    showing us God's hopes and truths;
celebrating good potential
    right amongst excluded youths?

Who is Christ if not an artist
    drawing us towards the sands;
celebrating humble wisdom
    loos'ning stones from hearts and hands?

Who is Christ if not a dancer
    blessed by women, hurt by men;
celebrating hope's defiance,
    helping life to rise again?

Who is Christ if not the beggar
    longing to be shown some love;
celebrating human kindness
    from below? Praise God above!

Who is Christ if not all children
    asking 'why?' when life's unfair;
celebrating dreams of justice
    moulding action – if we dare?

Who is Christ if not our neighbour –
    friend or stranger, old or young;
celebrating God's embracing
    you and me and everyone!

Graham Adams
England

Rural Hope

God, give hope.
Give hope to the couple,
far beyond retirement age,
driving their cattle to milking,
with no one to follow them.
God, give hope.

Give hope to young people
looking for somewhere they can
afford to live.
God, give hope.

Give hope to migrant labourers,
working hard in the fields,
far from their home earth.
God, give hope.

Give hope to people working
in the tourist trade,
at the mercy of forces
outside their control.
God, give hope.

God, give hope to the land.
Let your kingdom come on the earth.

Bob Warwicker
England

Learning Hope

The reflections of a community priest on lessons learned from the poor about where to find God and about 'hope'. Susan was responsible for a group of theological students working in a disadvantaged multicultural neighbourhood in Auckland, Aotearoa New Zealand.

I learned about hope amongst people called 'hopeless'.
I was with them as minister and priest.
'God' was my trade.

I was peddling 'hope', selling shares in the future, insuring
    life:
So I thought!

Convinced I was that hope in Jesus
The Way, the Christ, the Bread of life
Was their answer.
An invitation to banqueting tucked in my briefcase,
An answer to need in my prayer.

I had seen breakfast, and lunch and dinner:
Poverty and powerlessness and disappointment the meals
    served up.
Hopelessness was fluffy slippers, was pink candlewick,
    was gas oven.

I learned about hope from people called 'hopeless'.
No Jesus dying – too much pain, we've seen it before.
No promised future – too long, too costly, no return, we're
    forgotten.

Here, now, today is what matters!
Chips, sausages, taro, chop-suey
Rent for the flat, dollars for shopping, 'A' grades at school
A 'yes please' and 'thank you'
Children at school, partner home sober, a yard clear of
    wrecks …
What was I hearing!

I learned about hope amongst people called 'hopeless'.
Hope here and now, seen in daily achievement
Hope found in shoes in trousers and jersey
In pot on the stove and in food on the table
In voiced invitation to eat.

Now, hope's in our listening, our anger, our tears.
No Bible, no prayer, no pious assurance.
And God?
The bread on the table
The hope for today.

Susan Adams
Aotearoa New Zealand

Hope Where Are You?

I especially need to know your face when I feel you slipping or crashing away from me. The old me feels that I should still experience you inside and beside me. But I seem to lose you when I see new forms of military might, and oppression of indigenous peoples and people living with grinding poverty forming and reforming in my lifetime. When oppression feels very close to my personal being and security, my questions about you are very practical.

I think I may have come to terms with the idea that there is no fixed and final state of perfection on earth, not only in my lifetime, but ever. But that makes me ask even more questions about who you are, and how I find you and recognise you. I know there may be no final answers but I demand a conversation.

I need to remind us both who I am as we speak. I have many identities. I am a single woman, a migrant of British origin and a priest. I have lived in Aotearoa, New Zealand for 43 years. I am deeply committed to justice in this land.

Hope, I am wondering, if you are in the struggle, rather than a pre-determined end. Hope, perhaps you are not in opposition to hopelessness. Perhaps you have a mysterious inter-dependence.

Hope, perhaps you give multiple births to yourself. Perhaps the faces of your twins and triplets will always be shaped by nature, nurture, experience, and environment. Perhaps you create a plethora of possible forms of healthy community to which we are becoming blind in our loss of imagination as we focus in on ourselves as 'lords' of the universe.

Hope, you have many faces, so we may not immediately recognise you. The uniqueness of each of your faces depends on where we are collectively standing in society in terms of power, privilege and influence. Your faces will be fully present among oppressed groups. You will also be among us who are part of the dominant force in society. Our first reaction to you may be joy or collective shame depending on what you have to say to us. But once we see what you need from us, we could nurture you with the passionate feather-like touch that calls forth life from a tiny premature baby.

I live in a world of contradictions: violence and beauty, fear and courage. I know that I am capable of stubbornly assuming that you, hope, will be re-born in every possible situation. I refuse to believe that fragile hope will finally die.

So, for now, I'll go on living and learning, especially from those who seem to me to have less grounds for hope than I.

Jean Brookes
Aotearoa New Zealand

Hope in the Lord

(Blessed is the one who trusts in the Lord,
and whose hope the Lord is. Jeremiah 17.7)

Creator God
we look at the sea, whose tide unfailingly ebbs and flows
the times governed by the moon;
we look at the sun, rising each morning heralding the day
setting each evening shepherding in the night;
the circle of seasons continues despite our misuse of the
    planet.

Creator God
forgive our doubts
please help us to trust in you.

Loving Jesus, you spent your short life giving hope
to those you healed
to those who mourned
to those who were rejected.
You gave your life and death, that we may have hope today
hope for ourselves
hope for each other
hope for the world.

Hope that this life is not the end, but the beginning
of life in your kingdom – starting now.

Loving Christ
in the times when we feel hopeless
please help us to find our hope in you.

Embracing Spirit
fill us with your peace and power
that our lives may shine with the reflected love of Jesus;
even as our hope is in him,
so may his hope be in us
to bring joy and light
into the corner of the world in which we live.

Heather Johnston
Scotland

Opportunities

Opportunities
occur
to all
who grasp
as given
the hope to know
the things to grow
the things to show
that heaven
on earth

is now
to seize
as we receive
gifts to perceive
love to conceive.

David J. Harding
England

Rich Fool

'Four Rolls Royces,
three Mercedes Benz,
two Lamborghini
safe within their pens.

The Rovers are all over.
Porsches are in the shed.
How I love to count my cars
while lying in my bed.

Bentleys are in the annexe
with a Jaguar or two,
but if they send that Cadillac,
then what am I to do?

I'll build a bigger garage.
Then the neighbours' eyes will pop ...'
But precisely at that moment
God said, 'Stop!'

Marjorie Dobson
England

Just One Year

(Luke 12.13–21)

God of Life, Creator of the earth and all that is in it, we lift
   our prayers of thanks to you
For the beauty of the earth that surrounds us,
For spring flowers that dazzle us and summer's greenery
   that delights us,
For autumn's bounty that sustains us, and winter's
   hibernation which settles us.

**Thanks be to You, Lord of the heavens and the earth, to
whom all things belong.**

God, we enjoy your abundance, yet are seduced by
   accumulation.
The mantra, 'More is better', lulls us.
New inventions become seeming 'necessities'.
We fill our cupboards and closets, basements and barns to
   overflowing.
Yet we despair, feeling our lives stand empty.

God, let us not be possessed by our possessions.

God, we claim to enjoy your peace, yet we persist in worry
   about things.
Even as Scripture reminds us that Solomon's finery cannot
   compare to the flowers of the fields, we worry about our
   house, our car – our cars, our clothes, our shoes.
Yet we despair, sensing our coveted treasures bring no
   lasting meaning to life.

God, let us not be possessed by our possessions.

God, we sing of your 'blessed assurance', yet crave
   promises from our banks and pensions.
We worry if our Individual Retirement Accounts will see us
   through.

We store up more and more riches for our earthly security.
Yet we despair, discovering we are not 'rich towards' you.

God, let us not be possessed by our possessions.

God, we commit ourselves to care for others,
Yet we stock our pantries for tomorrow, while millions
suffer empty bellies today.
We focus on our shoe collection while millions go bare-
footed.
We lament our fashion follies while others lament that their
children go naked and cold.
We deposit ever more into our bank accounts while
millions live from day to day.

God, let us not be possessed by our possessions.

God, our life span is short, at any moment to be taken from
us.
Free us from greed, and fill us with generosity.
Release us from insecurity and restore us to contentment
with the treasures of your kingdom.
Strip us of our fear and strengthen us to love one another as
you have loved us.
In Jesus' name we lift our prayers to you.

**Thanks be to you, Lord of the heavens and the earth, to
whom all things belong. Amen.**

Tod and Ana K. Gobledale
Australia/USA

6

Worshipping the God of Hope

Life-giving God

Life-giving God, source of all love,
Your energy and creative spirit fill the earth!
Through you we dare to hope
    for a fiesta in which all people will join,
With you we dare to search
    for a new song to be sung by the whole earth,
In you we dare to dream
    of the liberation which Christ has promised.
Amen.

Chris Esdaile and Alison Facey
Chile/England

Inspirational God

Inspirational God,
we may not always feel like singing,
but when we catch the spirit of your song
it inspires us to sing along with you.
Thank you for all the beauty and energy
and the vitality of the music
of your creative power and your love.
Teach us how to be in tune with you more often,
because it is a wonderful feeling
to have something to sing about
and to join with others in our singing.

Marjorie Dobson
England

Tender God

Tender God,
Your justice is our peace;
Your peace is our hope;
Your presence, our delight!
Give us this day and always,
A bread of freedom to share,
A cup of hope to pour upon the earth.
Amen.

United Society for the Propagation of the Gospel
England

God Give Us Hope

(Opening Responses)

God of hope, who calls creation into being
Open our eyes to the vision of heaven on earth.
God of hope, embodied in our daily living
Set our faces to seek your purpose.
God of hope, who inspires our breathing,
Set our hearts on fire with a desire for justice.

God, give us your hope

When we become passive,
resigned to waiting, despairing of change,
God, give us the impatient hope
that calls us to act with you.

When we become too comfortable,
accepting the trivial and the mundane,
God, give us the restless hope
that stirs us to change with you.

When we are over-anxious,
desperate to find solutions,

God, give us the quiet hope
that rests, trusting, in you.

When we are overwhelmed by grief
and the pain of the world seems too much to bear
God, give us the enduring hope
that finds its source and goal in you.

When we put our hope in illusions,
relying on easy security and glib assurances
God, give us the true hope
that is founded on your promise.

Jan Berry
England

Let Us Worship Together

Friends, let us worship together.
Once again affirm our faith in God.
God who created us is here with us
Surrounding us with his love and grace.

The crucified Christ is here with us
Sharing our sorrows, fear and pain.
The risen Christ is here with us
Assuring us of victory over evil again.

So, in the midst of fear and terror
Let us find our hope in God alone
When distorted faiths trigger violence
Let the true faiths break silence.

Let us sow the seeds of love
Let us reap the joy of fellowship
Let us pray for each other now
And together praise and worship.

Elizabeth Joy
South India/England

As We Meet to Offer Worship

As we meet to offer worship
God will fill the life we live
with the passion of the sunrise,
offering all so we can give.

Born through God, through God we offer
fierce compassion, fervent praise;
giving back to God, in goodness,
love through every faltering phrase;

Love that shuns the world's indifference,
love that never questions why
in the search for full communion
God holds sway and self will die.

Lost to self, to God we offer
through each one we face each day,
all that love can gift or proffer
all we are, or think, or say.

Tune: Metre 8.7.8.7

Andrew Pratt
England

Nothing is Impossible with God

The light of Christ out of the darkness springs –
Amazed acceptance touched by silent wings;
As all creation trembles at a child's first cry
God speaks in human history
His ever-lasting Word.

Meet with us, Lord, and take us by surprise –
Dispel our fantasies and make us wise;

Give us compassion, courage and integrity,
Immerse us in forgiveness,
Encircle us with peace.

Christ's power emboldens all who hear his call –
Renews resolve in those who faint or fall –
Makes possible the dreams that scarcely dare come true –
New challenges and choices
Wait for their time to come.

Instil in us such all-pervasive joy
That evil's worst intent shall not destroy.
Christ's hands hold fast the wounded world in all its pain;
Unquenched by human hatred
Light out of the darkness springs.

Jill Jenkins
England

Our Living and Challenging God

Our living and challenging God,
you keep every promise you make.
You offer your Spirit and word
and call on your people to speak.
We open our hearts and our hands
and ask for your wisdom and skill,
that we may be sound in our plans
and ready to follow your will.

We offer the vision of youth,
our courage and quickness of mind,
our power to be stung by the truth
and follow each challenge we find.
Don't let us react without thought
or take everything at a run,
but add to the vision we've caught
a talent for getting things done.

We offer the wisdom of years,
the precious potential to dream.
Acquainted with laughter and tears,
we carefully value each scheme.
Don't let us get set in our ways,
or harden our hearts to the new,
but drawn from the length of our days,
help us show the right thing to do.

We wait for your Spirit to fall
on women and children and men,
that we may respond to your call,
be filled with your power, and then,
with actions inspired by the truth
and words that confront people's lies,
together in age and in youth,
we offer the length of our lives.

Janet Wootton
England

God of Creativity

God of Creativity
We come sitting,
Standing,
Dancing
before you
    with our dreams and hopes
    knowing that you are a God of Love.

We praise you
    for being in our dreams and hopes
    maybe a new design for decorating a room
        perhaps a new friend
        a new football or computer game
            better ideas for
Loving
Caring

Sharing for people
in our community
for being alongside people
a determination to bring about
change for a more
Just Society.

We are sorry that we have destroyed
Enthusiasm
Dashed dreams when people
have rushed up to us
full of their new ideas
Hopes
Dreams
Shattered
and we have upset a life with just one look
or a sharp word
because of a lack of vision
or selfishness.

Creating God
You know
and we know
that all the time Creativity
is there to be
developed
but you know
and we know
that we do not always dance
even when we hear the music.

So, Dancing God
Move us to dance to the tune
that will bring in
Heaven on Earth.
Amen.

Geoffrey Duncan
England

How Can the Time of Peace Come to Earth?

How can the time of peace come to earth?
When will the bomb be banned?
How can true justice blossom in mirth?
When will the violence end?
      Hidden within your heart and mine
      Lie all the answer's parts:
      Peace is a lake vibrant with gold –
      Peace starts within our hearts.
Cherish the dream, yes cherish the hope,
Dance in the face of death:
Friends join with me to work for true peace –
Honour each person's worth.

Peace without justice withers and dies –
War will forever be
'Til all the poor gain power and land,
'Til all the poor are free.

      Look to the poor, look to the child,
      Ponder the truths they hold;
      Answers of gold nurtured with love –
      Wisdom for young and old.
Cherish their dreams, yes cherish their hopes,
Dance with God's life not death;
Stand with the poor and stand with the child –
Honour each person's worth.

Who can sustain this struggle for peace
Lacking true peace within?
Love which embraces those who would kill
Springs from self-love within.
      God made us all, God loves us all –
      Loves us despite our wrongs.
      Come and affirm your worth and mine,
      Sing worth in all our songs.

Cherish the dream, yes cherish the hope,
Dance in the face of death.
Friends let us work for Justice and Peace –
Bring God's new world to birth!

W. L. Wallace
Aotearoa New Zealand

Holy Spirit, Sudden Gust

Holy Spirit, sudden gust
   and darting tongue of flame,
one whose presence is a must
   or worship's limp and lame,
as we gather here to meet,
come, and sweep us off our feet,
where we're cold, turn up the heat –
   it's new creation time!

Holy Spirit, gentle dove,
   all-animating breath,
you bear fruit in peace and love,
   you bring life out of death,
draw together those apart
with your reconciling art,
stimulate the stony heart –
   it's new creation time!

Holy Spirit, one of three,
   the God who goes between,
you declared the Jubilee
   through God the Nazarene,
through the church communicate
words and deeds that liberate,
and the world will be a fête –
   it's new creation time!

Tune: Kelvingrove

Kim Fabricius
Wales/USA

Green Woodpecker

Poets and bird books
have called you: hecco,
hewel, hick-quail,
popinjay, wodewale

but last Sunday
driving out early from the DIY store,
when I saw you flutter
between two spindly trees,
caught in a spool of sun
in the car park –

I knew you by your
green carpenter's apron,
your red-crested head –
and watching you chisel bark
with all the care of a craftsman
in the pearled heat,

I heard you tapping out
a morning prayer.

Denise Bennett
England

The Dance

I watch the dance each day
of the morning sun on the sea.
I hear and watch the instruments
all along the way.

We all dance on this path
the tuba, French horn,
the big bass drum
playing tunes, dancing song.

I behold Divine connection
we are all one
in the dance of this universe

the words alive before me
you can't separate the dance from the dancer:
immersed in the sea of the 'Divine'.

Eleanore Milardo
USA

Enthusiastic Hope that Broadens Expectation

The cosmos is revolving with endless rhythmic rhyme,
the circle keeps on turning to mark off chances and time;
and through the life we're living and images we see,
we plot the hopeful story of God's eternity.

The summer sheds its harvest as autumn turns to gold,
the springtime and its newness is lost in time, grown old;
the cold of winter beckons, the trees are crippled, bare,
but seeds of hope are hidden, await the spring's repair.

This broadens expectation, the life for which we hope,
the gift of resurrection, the faith for which we grope,
are found within our compass and not beyond our grasp,
these gifts of grace and loving are sown in us to last.

Andrew Pratt
England

Hope

On a solemn grey afternoon
I strode across a muddy field
Be-booted, be-gloved, looking for life.

The wood edge was dull with bare, brown trees
Grey birds fluttered at my feet –
Then a flash of sunlight swept across the vale
Enflaming the tree tops, bursting red with buds.

As soon, the brightness faded,
Some heavenly light switch flicked off,
But the potential of spring had been seen.

Sarah Ingle
England

Christmas Bliss

There is joy in my life
bubbling up, tickling my nose
champagne sparkling.
New-born lambs
in sunlight beneath
a snow-clothed mountain, wild waves pounding
a surf beach
blood tingling,
feet dancing.
Faint sound of bells
on Alpine cows,
Christmas bliss,
little children singing
'Away in a manger',
breaking the ice of mid-winter.
Hot chocolate and mince pies
after Midnight mass.
Or in another hemisphere
croissants and strawberries
for breakfast.
Stars reflected in a deep pool
take me to the depths of wonder.

A fiery sun leaping the horizon at dawn,
a sliver of silver against a black sky.
Effervescent delight.

Wendy d Ward
Aotearoa New Zealand

First Remembered Christmas

If I look through the window
I can see a little girl curled asleep
on a mattress, the floorboards are bare.
There are three small presents
at her feet:
some sweets,
some pretend money
and a fairy doll dressed in silver.

When she wakes
there is no smell of tangerines
or pine, no Christmas tree
to delight her – only the delight
in her tiny hands,
her shining eyes.

The sweets she quickly eats,
the money, she spends
a million times
but the magic of that fairy doll
she carries with her – all her life.

Denise Bennett
England

A New Hopefulness

(A responsive Act of Commitment)

God, give me the courage
to change what can be changed,
the serenity to accept what cannot,
and the wisdom to know the difference.
So help us all courageously
to pursue the demands of justice
in solidarity with all who long for it;
to build a community of grace
in solidarity with all who need it;
and to nurture godly wisdom
in solidarity with all who hide their own,
this day and for evermore.

Amen.

Graham Adams
England

A City Where All Share the Feast

A city where night never falls,
a peaceful garden where the dawn
forever breaks in splendour bright
and shines upon a world new born:
Jerusalem – your song we raise,
beyondness in our midst we praise.

A city where all share the feast
there truth and mercy both embrace,
there peace and justice both join hands,
there spring the fountains of your grace.
The light in whom we see the light
outpour in rivers of delight.

A city compassed round by song
where life is in its fullness found
a place where broken lives are healed
and praises evermore resound.
Spirit by whom the veil is torn
reveal the Lamb upon the throne.

David Fox
Wales

Litany of Hope in Solidarity

The Word became the hungry child with empty eyes and
swollen belly. We are his hope that one day his belly will be
filled with good things and the rich sent away empty.

Lord, give us grace to see
And faith to respond.

The Word became the poor who live amongst the garbage
the rich throw away. We are their hope that one day justice
will prevail and equality will be born.

Lord, give us grace to see
And faith to respond.

The Word became the war widow fleeing her savaged
country with six children and six plastic bags. We are her
hope that one day the mighty will be put down from their
thrones and her home will be rebuilt.

Lord, give us grace to see
And faith to respond.

The Word became the skeletal man, wracked by AIDS and
shunned by all. We are his hope that one day treatment will
be given and understanding will be his.

209

**Lord, give us grace to see
And faith to respond.**

The Word became the young girl prostituting her body to
keep her baby alive. We are her hope that one day the good
news of great joy will mean she can feed and clothe her
child.

**Lord, give us grace to see
And faith to respond.**

The Word became the orphan boy, bewildered and
confused. We are his hope that one day the war will be over
and peace will be won.

**Lord, give us grace to see,
faith to respond
And wisdom to receive from those to whom we give.**

Annabel Shilson-Thomas/CAFOD
England

Stainbeck

*The words of the following hymn were written for Stainbeck
United Reformed Church, Leeds, to celebrate the launch of The
Three Churches Project, an ecumenical community arts-based
initiative, and the induction of the Revd Angela Hughes as the
minister at Stainbeck. They are based on Jeremiah 32.1–15 and
Matthew 13.44–45. The story of this church and its outreach into
the local community is one of hope, for it demonstrates what can be
achieved when the people of God refuse to be overwhelmed by
decline and decay and try to find new ways of being the Church. At
a time of shared sorrow following the death of their minister's
younger son in the Tsunami disaster, and at a time of tension and
anxiety within the city of Leeds after the London bombings, this
small church took a bold step to reach out in faith and love to the
people whom they seek to serve.*

Like the prophet Jeremiah
when he bought his cousin's field,
we will show by word and action
that our hopes will never yield,
for the future of God's promise
is for ever signed and sealed.

Like the man who found the treasure
hidden deep beneath the earth,
or the merchant in his longing
for a pearl of matchless worth,
we will give our utmost efforts
to proclaim the kingdom's birth.

As the prophets of God's kingdom,
As co-workers in God's field,
we will never cease from striving
for God's love to be revealed.
We will show by word and action
how the wounds of life are healed.

On mean streets of strife and hatred,
where the gun or bomb is 'boss',
in the midst of life's disasters
we will not be drowned by loss.
We will show by word and action,
God in Christ upon the cross.

Praise to Father, Son and Spirit,
God our Maker, Brother, Friend,
God, whose hopes for human nature
cannot be brought to an end,
God, upon whose faithful promise
we for ever will depend.

Tune: Oriel or Westminster Abbey

Jean Mortimer
England

211

Harvest

Lord of the Harvest,
you share your wealth with us in creation
and show us the abundance of your generosity
in the fruits of the earth.

As we celebrate your great goodness
fill us with your gift of life
that through love outpoured
we may be instruments of your compassion.

Give us eyes to see your face in the needs of others
and ears to hear your voice in the cries of the poor
that with arms outstretched we may let go of our riches
and share the earth's bounty with all your people.

Fill us with longing for a world made whole
and ignite in us a fire for justice
that we may strive to see the hungry filled
and work together to make poverty history.

Give us courage to transform the past
and hope to share the future
that lands once parched and dry
may bring forth fruit for all.
Amen.

Annabel Shilson-Thomas/CAFOD
England

Multi-faith Food Blessing

We eat and drink these fruits of earth,
that love may grow between us all,
between us all.

We join God's holy cause and share our
bread with all the poor of earth,
the poor of earth.

To God whom many faiths adore
be praises now and evermore
and evermore.

W. L. Wallace
Aotearoa New Zealand

Creative Creator

Lord of Life,
Creator of Communities,
    enable me
    to read the gospels with a new understanding,
    to see the world around me set within a global context,
    to appreciate people for who they are and
    to love humankind in a more positive way.

Lord of Life
Spirit of Creativity
    encourage me
    to step out into the world with a new vision,
    to accept challenges and speak out for justice,
    to expect positive action as a normal part of life and
    to bring benefits to women, men and children,

for improving relationships with people
as Christ would have us do.
Amen.

Geoffrey Duncan
England

Hope Has a Heartbeat

Hope has a heartbeat,
   a light step
   a ready smile
   an easy laugh.

It is the living words who give me hope:
   embodied souls,
     heaven-kissed
     and heaven-bent,
   who embrace day and night
   with courage and joy,
   who tell the truth
   regardless of the cost,
   whose lives speak of grace
   and shine with the reflected glow

of a God who never gives up on us.

Carla A. Grosch-Miller
England/USA

Amid the Many Thoughts

Amid the many thoughts
Of what we might become
What images can help us live
With lively hope and fun?
Should heroes fill our minds
With conflicts and with wars
Pronouncing what they see as ills
To be life's only cause?

Perhaps a clown would suit
With sad or happy face

214

Whose thinking tumbles upside down
Within God's laughing space?
Would feudal king or lord
Be our best frame of mind?
Should pyramids of wealth and pow'r
Be sought for or declined?

Or should the victim role
The one whom others used
Allow our power to be assigned
Our worth to be abused?
Beyond the powerless role
Beyond rebellion's space
Beyond oppressor's use of pow'r
We find the Christ-child's face.

May strong ones feel their wounds
May meek ones own their fire
May all crusaders learn to laugh
And sing within God's choir.
O God who comes in peace
As nurture and support
Help us to choose the Jesus Way
Of actioned love and thought.

Tune: Roslyn or Ich Halte Treulich Still

W. L. Wallace
Aotearoa New Zealand

Radiance

He kissed my eyes
and I awoke, still drowsy.
Stretching arms and legs and back
I arose, puzzled.

I did not know I had been asleep
until he came by.
How odd only to know
when his lips brushed open my eyes.
Perhaps it was a different kind of sleep,
not the sleep of night,
rather the sleep of lack of light.

Then the moment came,
when he passed by
and saw my darkened eyes.
Bending over, his radiant face
chased away all sleep.
With a quiet sigh, he breathed
over me and said,
'Night is over, dawn has broken.
Arise, precious one and come with me.
What was hidden is revealed,
where there were shadows
now there is light.'
'Yes, I want to come
but my slumbers have been long,
my body is chilled and numb.'
He pressed gentle fingers over my heart,
warmth flowed through veins
until I tingled with life again.
I remembered a monastery garden,
a snowdrop, white and pure,
growing out of bare, cold earth.
I thought of love that gives light,
warmth and hope.

Wendy d Ward
Aotearoa New Zealand

Easter Vitality

Lord Jesus, set my heart on doing good –
merrily and eagerly,
tenderly and carefully,
madly and passionately –
with all the gladness that flooded the great, green earth
with heart and healing
on that Sunday when life came leaping from the tomb.
Amen.

Peter Graystone
England

I Saw the Gardener Dancing

(John 20.15)

I saw the gardener dancing
The cross became a tree –
A tree that blooms in springtime
With Easter ecstasy
It signs the way of wholeness –
For heart and loins and head,
And grows beside the pathway
To life when all seems dead.

When markets cast their shadows
And fix with icy gaze
Our wisdom names the blindness
That kills our dancing days.
When people change direction,
When spirit's needs are fed
We move beyond consuming
The crusts of market bread.

Come flow with rhythmic motion,
Be like a dancing tree.

Come join the springtime flowing
That sets the spirit free.
Embrace the gardener's sequence
Of dormant need to flower
'Til all our hearts are growing
And Easter comes each hour.

W. L. Wallace
Aotearoa New Zealand

Joys to Come

In the language of flowers
Celandines mean:
'Joys to come'.

It is late January, hardly Spring,
yet already a few heads
begin to show.

Already the warmth of my words
penetrate; the silence
begins to thaw.

Denise Bennett
England

Go from Here Full of Hope

And so we prepare to leave this place,
and the earth keeps turning, hurtling through space,
and darkness falls and daylight dawns in one land and
    another.
So let us hold in our prayers all people –
waking, sleeping, being born, and dying –
one world, one humanity,
forever changing, forever the same.
Let us go from here full of hope –

as people who live in the light,
secure in the knowledge that light has shone in darkness,
and the darkness will never master it,
and eager, in the company of Jesus Christ,
the righteous one,
to walk a bright path through time.
Amen.

Peter Graystone
England

Easter Blessing

(Based on Psalm 118.22–29, Matthew 28.1–10, John 21.4–14)

As we go on our way,
we know we will face other earthquakes in our lives,
but we shall also meet angels with good news.
As we go on our way,
we know there will be more rejection in people's lives,
but we can help to turn it into resurrection.
As we go on our way,
we remember the brokenness of the Last Supper,
but the Easter Breakfast makes things whole again,
in the power of God's love, alive for all people,
this day, tomorrow and for ever.
Amen.

Graham Adams
England

Feed Nations with Your Love

(Ecumenical Worship)

From all faiths and beliefs we come
strung together by concerns for the world,
here to touch each worry lightly
in quiet prayer or shared worship –

each of us burdened a little by our journey.
Lord, sustain us with your Word.
Feed nations with your Love.

Eve Jackson
England

Come by Here

The words of 'Kum ba ya' are sung by the congregation to lead into each section of this prayer.

All sing
'Kum ba ya, my Lord, Kum ba ya [3 times]
O Lord, Kum ba ya'

Leader
Come by here, Lord. Come to your people in this place as we worship together and let us be aware of your living presence.
Come to our sisters and brothers who, like us are gathered together for worship at this time. May they, too, know your living presence.
Come to the people of this town in all their varied activities today – out in the streets, on the sand, in the parks, at home, at work, relaxing, caring or receiving care. Be a living presence among the people in this town today.
Kum ba ya.

All sing
'Someone's crying, Lord, Kum ba ya [3 times]
O Lord, Kum ba ya'

Leader
Someone's crying , Lord – and you hear their cries. May we hear them too.
People are crying here and all over the world – crying in

grief and loneliness; crying out in fear, in hunger, in distress. You hear the cries of the homeless, the refugees, those who are unjustly treated and oppressed, those excluded from community, those denied access to the basic needs of life.
Someone's crying, Lord, Kum ba ya.

All sing
'Someone's praying, Lord, Kum ba ya [3 times]
O Lord, Kum ba ya'

Leader
Someone's praying, Lord – you hear their prayers – our prayers.
Guide us in our praying – make us ready to open our hearts to you – to listen as well as to speak, to place ourselves before you with all our faults and confess the hurt we have caused to others. Guide us in our praying, so that we may know forgiveness. We place ourselves before you in silence …
Someone's praying, Lord, Kum ba ya.

All sing
'Someone's singing, Lord, Kum ba ya [3 times]
O Lord, Kum ba ya'

Leader
Someone's singing, Lord – songs of joy as well as songs of sorrow; songs of love as well as songs of hurt; songs of hope as well as songs of pain.
We offer *our* songs, our love and our hope and trust that out of death comes life as we seek to follow in your Way.

Amen.

Wendy Ross-Barker
England

Candles

Candles on a living stone,
light to shine me home,
light to show me where to go,
light to help me know
    what is right and
    what is wrong and
that people all belong one to another
    sisters, brothers,
    sons and daughters on the move
    carrying their tents of love
    through the darkness,
    desert starkness,
    to the shining of a light
    in the deepest night,
light within God's living stone,
candle set to light me home.

Colin Ferguson
England

Shining with Hope

Holy Spirit of God,
light a flame within me,
burning for justice,
glowing with kindness,
shining with hope
for the end of poverty
and the peace of all people
in this ever-turning world.
Amen.

Peter Graystone
England

Benediction for Hope

May God, the Creator of hope,
challenge you to see hope in every situation.

May the Christ, hope embodied,
inspire you to bring hope to others.

And may the Spirit, who stirs hope within us,
move you to act according to her light.

Louise Margaret Granahan
Canada

Evening Prayer

Thank you God for night sounds;
frogs singing in the spring,
crickets chirping to their mates,
dry leaves rustling,
winter winds howling,
the plaintive call of a train whistle,
the wail of a siren,
the sound of my own breath.
God, you are in the night sounds.
Tune my ears to the pitch of your voice
calling to me in the darkness.
Amen.

Carol Penner
Canada

God Be with You

God be with you and to bless you.
God use other hands to hold you.
God will carefully enfold you.
God will grant you peaceful sleeping.
God will greet you when awaking.

Marjorie Dobson
England

Closing Blessing

May the God who gives hope go with you,
upholding you with courage and love,
until heaven comes on earth
and all creation shouts for joy.
Amen.

Jan Berry
England

Walk with Us

Loving God
　　walk with us we move out from our security.
Compassionate Christ
　　motivate us to take risks like Jesus.
Spirit of God
　　re-assure
　　re-new
　　and re-commit us to a life of service
　　with no strings attached
　　where we will live for justice and peace.

Geoffrey Duncan
England

7

Christ Our Eternal Hope

True Happiness

Christ is the hope of the world.
He gives direction to those who feel lost.
He gives purpose to those who lack aims.
He never fails those who call for help.

Christ is the hope of the world.
He leads people from the valley of darkness.
He encourages folk in the pit of despair.
He rescues many from the pain of loneliness.

Christ is the hope of the world.
Where there is conflict, he brings harmony.
Where there is war, he brings peace.
Where there is hate, he brings love.

Christ is the hope of the world.

John Johansen-Berg
England

Jesus is Risen

Jesus is risen,
raised by the Father,
and the imprisoned
rise in his train;

hell has been harrowed,
evil defeated;
humankind, hallowed,
shares in his reign.

Jesus is living,
ruling from heaven
through his forgiving
people on earth;
churches in mission
groan with creation,
hastening fruition,
cosmic rebirth.

Jesus is coming,
time for rejoicing,
heavens are humming,
planets and stars;
foes are befriended,
friends are astonished,
hands are extended,
bearing the scars.

Then Jesus, handing
over the kingdom –
everyone standing,
cheering the Lord –
gives all his glory
back to the Father,
ending the story
Scripture records.

Tune: Addington

Kim Fabricius
Wales/USA

When Easter Rays Shine Out

When Easter rays shine out
And warm the coldest heart
Then love breaks through and lives
And alleluias start
Alleluia, alleluia,
Let Easter alleluias start.

When Easter fills sad hearts
With promise and surprise
Then hope breaks through and lives
And alleluias rise
Alleluia, alleluia,
Let Easter alleluias rise.

When bruised and damaged ones
Christ's truth and justice know
Then peace breaks through and lives
And alleluias grow
Alleluia, alleluia,
Let Easter alleluias grow.

When all, set free from fear,
Can celebrate and sing
Then joy breaks through and lives
And alleluias ring
Alleluia, alleluia,
Let Easter alleluias ring.

Tune: St John (Adoration)

Wendy Ross-Barker
England

Easter Litany

Risen Christ,
when darkness overwhelms us
may your dawn beckon.

When fear paralyses us
may your touch release us.

When grief torments us
may your peace enfold us.

When memories haunt us
may your presence heal us.

When justice fails us
may your anger ignite us.

When apathy stagnates us
may your challenge renew us.

When courage leaves us
may your spirit inspire us.

When despair grips us
may your hope restore us.

And when death threatens us
may your resurrection light lead us.

Annabel Shilson-Thomas/CAFOD
England

Easter

Where life and love are blossoming
And tear-drenched eyes grow clear
Then alleluias will be sung
By lips long closed by fear.

Where hate-filled hearts are changed by love
Where peace its gladness brings
Then life breaks out in place of death
And joy from sorrow springs.

Unlock the doors we hide behind
And speak your words of peace
Break through all sadness and all fear
Your strength in us release.

Then send us out, encouraged by
The spirit you will give
To unlock doors in all the world
That all may fully live.

Tune: Dorking or St Stephen (Newington)

Wendy Ross-Barker
England

Resurrection NOW!

It wasn't easy to
> *forge a nation out of a handful of nomads,*
> *build the Church out of a mixed bag of Jews and Gentiles,*
> *bear good news as a group of grieving women:*
> *these narratives were born to give life*
> *to people facing death.*
Experiences of people seeking new life set us free to pray:

Word of Life,
we seek resurrection now.
We know terror and distress
take our words away when we hear
> 'Do what I say and you won't be hurt',
> 'Don't tell anyone our little secret',
> 'Shut up or it'll really hurt next time',
in our body-numbing, person-crushing, encounters.

Roller of Stones,
we seek resurrection now.
We are immobilised into inactivity
by such very large stones,
yet sometimes we are alarmed
when they begin to roll away
and new life is there to be claimed.

Risen Christ,
we seek resurrection now.
One with us in life and in death,
move us on
to meet you and greet you
as resurrected people
NOW!

Janet Lees
England

Risen Lord

Risen Lord,
shed your light on those who live in the shadow of death
and warm the hearts of those who have lost hope
that they who daily bear the cross of hunger
may find your Promised Land
and move from slavery to freedom.
As we proclaim your Easter song
help us to die to greed and rise to justice,
to abandon apathy and take up action
that rich and poor together may travel the road to freedom
and be restored to your resurrection life. Amen.

Annabel Shilson-Thomas/CAFOD
England

Easter Hope

God, whom we meet in bread and wine,
in body broken and love outpoured,
fill us with your compassion
that we may hear the cries of the hungry
and reach out to those in need.
Engender in us a thirst for justice
that the hungry will be satisfied
and the rich sent empty away.
Roll away our apathy
that, with arms outstretched,
we may offer life in place of death
and hope in the face of despair.
Amen.

Annabel Shilson-Thomas/CAFOD
England

Living and Dying

It is hard to believe, God,
the notion of resurrection.
Death is very real.

Here is the bundle of exquisitely sewn clothes
made with such love, still with her smell and feel,
but now her hands lie quiet
on her dead breast.

Here is his place, his empty chair, his tools,
the half-made artefacts he will not now complete.
He lies in earth, strong arms untimely still,
his sisters desolate.

Here's where she spoke of justice, stood for truth
until one night they came for her with guns.
Her voice is still, her body broken
in some unmarked grave.

231

These are they who have passed through the great ordeal;
... God shall wipe every tear from their eyes.

God of all comfort,
wipe the tears from our eyes too.
Help us to see that the hard reality of death
is conquered by the love that lives for ever,
the faith that looks for glimpses of life and hope,
and the truth of God's good news of justice and love.
Through Jesus Christ, risen and alive today.

Heather Pencavel
England

That All May Fully Live

Where life and love are blossoming
And tear-drenched eyes grow clear
Then alleluias will be sung
By lips long closed by fear.

Where hate-filled hearts are changed by love
Where peace its gladness brings
Then life breaks out in place of death
And joy from sorrow springs.

Unlock the doors we hide behind
And speak your words of peace
Break through all sadness and all fear
Your strength in us release.

Then send us out, encouraged by
The spirit you will give
To unlock doors in all the world
That all may fully live.

Tune: Dorking or St Stephen (Newington)

Wendy Ross-Barker
England

On the Beach: Easter Sunrise

Leaving the car, I watch bladder wrack
celebrate the North Sea.
On the beach fractured shells
balance in Euclidean arcs:
details ravelled in design.

Prayer will not drown in this swell,
so I parcel veteran sorrows in words
of penitence. Waves scuff shingle
while I catalogue arrant times.
Silence stalls. Painful knots.

Lingering in eel grass at the edge
of light shapes thoughts of
– you, making our making
and feathers, bubbles, dark matter;
– you, an infant crying for Arcturus,
bringing a fresh-minted future;
– you, the simplicity of life,
nestling in oarweed and red dulse;
– you, love's puzzle, picking poppy
globes, distilling past and present;
– you, wedding my will to yours
in pain.

I find the map: though thoughts stay.
The car coughs, skidding on sea lettuce.
The village breakfasts in domestic homage.
Unable to paraphrase holiness, I tune
to Bruckner and wind up the window.

Dark blinds lift: no explanations.
Victory opens each fist.
Perhaps that's it.
Our only responsibility; to glorify.
To delight in him.

Derek Webster
England

233

Hope of Resurrection

When love is lost in death or separation
and cherished expectations seem but vain,
we turn to God for faith and consolation
expecting nothing, yet we hope again.

When in our minds the silence of dejection
re-echoes but the silence of the grave,
we turn to God and find in God's affection
renewing quiet, silence strong to save.

From cross and tomb to hope of resurrection
the peace of God can bless and heal from pain,
turns separation into faith's communion
turns us from death to this world's life again.

David Fox
Wales

Not Yet!

But not yet!
For this is a waiting time,
a strange and uncertain time:
a hard and painful time.
> We wait in faith.
> We know the tale.
> We know the truth.
> But still we wait.
The wait is heavy.
Death deals our knockout blow.

Silence

And now our Lord and rock laid low,
the hope Christ prompted withered.

We wait in faith.
We know the tale.
We know the truth.
But still we wait.
The Christ cut down, the cross still stands:
its rootless wood erect but dead,
a sacrifice for greater good,
the gallows grief is not the end.
We wait in faith
We know the tale.
We know the truth.
But still we wait.

Stephen Brown
Scotland

Though the Earthly Life ...

Though the earthly life of our friend has ceased
Though *her/his* body returns to dust
We celebrate *her/his* life with the song
Alleluia, Alleluia, Alleluia
Alleluia, Amen.

In *her/his* death as in life *she/he* shares the web
Of the cosmic cycles of God
Which celebrate all being with the song
Alleluia, Alleluia, Alleluia
Alleluia, Amen.

We shall keep treasured mem'ries in our minds
And let go of hurts from the past
To celebrate *her/his* life with the song
Alleluia, Alleluia, Alleluia
Alleluia, Amen.

Though our grief fills our eyes with tears of loss
Though our hearts are breaking with pain

We celebrate *her/his* life with the song
Alleluia, Alleluia, Alleluia
Alleluia, Amen.

We now join our voice to our friend's own song
As part of the song of the Earth
And sing with the sacred joy of God
Alleluia, Alleluia, Alleluia
Alleluia, Amen.

Tune: Departure Song

*Note: For use at a funeral the first three lines of each verse
can be sung as a solo with the congregation joining in the
chorus.*

W. L. Wallace
Aotearoa New Zealand

I Am the Resurrection and the Life

O Holy One, we have sealed off ourselves
– and others – from the resurrection-life
you make down-to-earth and human
in Jesus of Nazareth.
Inspire us, Holy One, to live
your way, your truth, your life that opens
our Good Fridays to your Easter Sunday –
   our This-is-the-end-of-everything
   to your In-the-end-a-new-beginning;
   our Nice-guys-finish-last
   to your The-last-shall-be-first;
   our Being-consumed-by-our-bread-seeking-life
   to your Being-sustained-by-your-life-giving-bread;
   our Demeaning-of-the-doubting-Thomas
   to your Discerning-of-the-honest-Thomas;
   our Breaking-and-making-our-Judases-bleed
   to your Breaking-and-bleeding-for-our-Judases.

236

O Holy One, help us roll away
our cynicism and despair
to open our Good Friday world
to your Easter light and air.

Norm S. D. Esdon
Canada

Our Hope of Freedom Beyond Death

Freedom from the encumbrance of our earthly bodies
enabling us to run faster than cheetahs
with more grace than gazelles,
to dance with feet that have no need to touch ground,
to laugh without fear of ensuing tears.

Freedom from the limitation of our minds
enabling us to have inspired thoughts
that transcend all earthly wisdom and knowledge,
to speak all known and unknown languages
with voices purer than a mountain stream.

Freedom from spiritual searching
as our souls soar higher than an eagle
winging their way home to Christ
who is perfect love and peace.

Heather Johnston
Scotland

Remembering

Some of the most beautiful things
in the world are small.

Often the most memorable moments
are with us for the shortest time.

The perfection of snowflakes, each one unique,
disappears with the warmth of a touch.

The bud opens fresh petals to bloom,
its scent carries on a breeze and is gone.

The vibrant colours of a rainbow
vanish as we approach.

A tiny life turns you upside down
leaving nothing but love.

Some of the most beautiful things
in the world are small.

Often the most memorable people
are with us for the shortest time.

To know them is to be touched
and to be touched is to remember.

Fiona Ritchie Walker
England

God Marks No Ending, Only New Beginnings

God marks no ending, only new beginnings,
until the consummation of our lives;
God keeps no count of losses, nor of winnings:
we move through grace, the holy spirit thrives.

So as we go beyond this time, this setting,
Rememb'ring all the laughter and the tears;
we go with God in faith, so not regretting
the moments shared, the hopes, the dreams, the fears.

Though parted for a while, we travel onward,
not knowing what the future has in store.
This phase will close, the spirit draws us forward,
we've tasted love, but God has promised more.

Tune: Intercessor

Andrew Pratt
England

Beginning

There are sands near your house

– where sandpipers stop in
   ribbon weeds to break
   winter's fast;

– where the sky's new fingers
   unscroll each day and thread
   life with memory;

– where arcs of white light surf
   skirl and scour shells
   for hope;

– where waves rinse
   old faith and sculpt
   new dreams;

– where sea and shingle
   draw strange motions:
   and I still cry for you;

– where exact tides
   drub bones,
   and bury vacant days;

– where I walk at the edge.
– And know – though
   you are gone –
   I can, I must,
   begin again.

Derek Webster
England

Crocus

With winter; death
Only to be reborn in spring
So not death; lying dormant
Like a waiting volcano,
Waiting for the sign,
First spring sunshine,
A new year.

Hannah Warwicker
England

Life

Fullness of life you came to give,
fullness of life you are.
I wait on you.

After the praises,
after the Word,
I wait on you.

You who know all things,
you who understand all things,
I wait

for that special word
of peace,
for that special touch
of life.

Giver of all, you give good gifts,
lover of all, you love into wholeness;
And so I wait on you.

Claire Smith
Guyana

Food That Lasts

In a hall in Lisbon, Portugal, where people with cerebral palsy eat,
there is a mural depicting the Last Supper.

Servant One,
    as you shared your last supper,
    so we share a meal that lasts,
        … and lasts,
        … and lasts.

Broken One,
    as your body was broken and
        you shared our suffering,
    so we, the broken and suffering,
        share the stuff of life.

Outpoured Love,
    as you poured out your blood
        in the promise of new life,
    so, as spit and sweat are poured out here,
        we work for renewed lives.

Sharing one,
    may the fellowship of your last supper
    infuse our lasting meal
    with your patience and persistence.

And as, here, we struggle
    to suck or chew and swallow,
    may we feed on you in our hearts
    by faith
    and with thanksgiving.

Janet Lees
England

241

The Wings of Hope

My hope
  Is in the caterpillar
  That became a butterfly.
My hope
  Is in the water bug
  That turned into a dragonfly.
My hope
  Is in the hidden star
  That shines in the darkest hour.
My hope
  Is in the love of God
  Which is our greatest power.
My hope
  Is in the Son of God
  Who turned water into wine.
My hope
  Is in the miracle
  That he becomes a friend of mine.
My hope is on the cross
  Where he gave his life for me.
My hope
  Is behind the stone
  From which he came to set me free.
Such hope,
  When water bug becomes a dragonfly
  When caterpillar becomes a butterfly
  And the old will die
  The new will fly
  With wings of beauty into the sky.
Yes, such hope,
  That as autumn follows summer
  And spring follows winter
  So day follows night

And life will follow death
In God's great mystery of creation.

Richard Becher
England

Hope Against Hope

He is standing at Dachau, in the snow with his fellow Jews
and in the furnace, with all who suffer, mankind. Beneath
the dark shadow that stunts us with fear, he is with us and in
the mushrooming cloud that disseminates our corruption,
he brings us news of a day beyond the eclipse, that he will
share with us.

Wherever we are, if we look, he is there beside us and
amid the falling of civilisations, will bind the broken spirit,
pouring oil in the wound and as from a cruse, hope, against
hope, in the mind.

Brian Louis Pearce
England

Mountains of Pain

When they blasted you
did you moan
did you writhe
in pain?

And when they carved you up
how did you feel
how did you bear it?

And when we
who 'now come'
decided that we
could dispense with you
who were always here
did you cry?

243

But we could not hide
your beauty,
only expose it.

Scars and wounds
of pain and beauty.

No shame.
No sorrow.

Only triumphant worship
of the relentless
god of progress.

Scars and wounds
Teach us . . .

The bird says,
'Winters do not last for ever.'
Pain ceases,
joy comes,
even now begins
nourished
by winter's chill and frost,
encouraged by spring's call,
summer's warmth.

It comes.

Claire Smith
Guyana

Loss of Hope

In bad times like this
we may be told to think of others who are worse off
and remember how Job was patient in suffering:
but this is not Job's trouble; it is all ours.

Because this trouble is ours, human trouble, it is also God's,
who took our nature and bore our sorrows.

Jesus loved those who came to him in their emptiness
and on the cross he was totally emptied and helpless.

He said, 'Take up your cross,' and it is heavy
but always in church there is the cross
and before he went to the cross he said, 'Thy will be done.'
It is hard for us to say it but he said it also for us.

After the cross there was life:
may we find from this point of death, a resurrection.

Raymond Chapman
England

The Promised Thing

Death.
Unknown and known.
Guaranteed at birth.
Promised for Any Day,
    Any Way,
    Come what may.

Death.
Feared and loathed,
Postponed and put off.
Promised for Any Day,
    Any Way,
    Come what may.

Promised for Any Day.
Perhaps in that is the fear.
Perhaps in the unknown
Lies its power.
    Any Way
    Come what may.

But death is known
In each death memory is grown.
In each death a seed is sown
For every other life.
    Many Ways
    For richer days.

Death.
Be it early or late,
Arriving in love or in hate,
The Promised Thing arrives.
    The Promised Thing
    In each death a life has been.

Death.
It need not be feared
Welcomed? Perhaps.
Greeted? Yes.
The promise made good,
The life affirmed, the memory stood.
    The Promised Thing.
    In each death a life has been.

Elizabeth Gray-King
England

Quaker Burial Ground

I stand at the foot
of a steep, green slope looking up;
everything is orderly,
headstones named and placed
against the walls –
do not expect to find kin –
Sarah Agnes Squire.

Here, in Abraham Darby's garden
the Iron masters of Coalbrookdale

and other Quakers sleep.
In the corner
a descendant from a tree,
under which George Fox once preached,
stammers into leaf.

But it is the giant redwoods
which take my breath;
two twin trees soaring,
tall as skyscrapers;
grown from a seed
the size of a tomato pip –

and below, the dissenters,
particles of self enrich the soil.
Atoms of what has gone and what will be
blown by the wind
to tremble on the bough.

Denise Bennett
England

Planting My Father

(for Sarah)

Planting my father
this afternoon
we sow his ashes
in a sunny spot by the wall
in the church garden of remembrance.

This is the place
I watched him as a child
using his strong hands
to till the land:
to weed and water,
order pansies and petunias.

Hands he used to pray
when I stood beside him on Sundays.

Here we bunch together
in pinks and lavenders,
like a family spray,
to think of him.

On this cold February day
I feel the heat
of his past conversations,
hoping that somewhere between
our flares and silences
we found a common ground;

knowing that his seed is rooted
in my own hands;
that when the sun warms the soil
in the spring, I will stoop
to cup the flowers –
to catch the scent
of his breath.

Denise Bennett
England

Now That I'm Gone

Don't forget the time we had together,
the plans you made and all you dreamed of.

Something in you changed
and all around you everything looked new.

Keep hold of all that was good
from my brief stay.

You carry something of me
everywhere you go.

Laugh and enjoy life,
make the most of each day.

Be the person you would
have wanted me to know.

Fiona Ritchie Walker
England

Prayer of Confession

Lord God
I am ashamed to confess
that just now, eternal hope seems very far away
a candle flame flickering in a strong breeze

violent crime, disease, natural disasters
so much of the world in which we live
seems to go against your loving, forgiving nature

sin, violence
hurricane and earthquake
powers we cannot control
bringing sadness and destruction

Forgive my doubt
my lack of faith and hope

At my lowest moments
remind me
that the life, death and resurrection of your Son Jesus
show how the hope offered by your everlasting love
can never be beaten or extinguished

Thanks be to you my God
Amen

Nick Butler
England

The Journey with Jesus the Refugee

This brief liturgy was originally written for a group of asylum seekers and refugees who visited Blackburn Cathedral during Refugee Week 2005 to walk The Journey, *a set of fifteen paintings by Penny Warden which re-interpret the traditional* Stations of the Cross *(adding a fifteenth 'Resurrection' station) within Blackburn's multi-faith context. While written with the paintings and the people involved in mind, this particular journey towards healing and hope could also be used together with other images as a public liturgy or as a private devotion walked with or in solidarity with refugees and asylum seekers. The introduction would need to be adjusted to suit the context.*

Introduction

We have come together to give thanks to God for *you* the refugees and asylum seekers of our community from many nations and cultures. We remember the journeys that have brought *you/them* to us, the journey which Jesus himself walked as a child refugee, as a critic of his own religion, as a citizen of an occupied territory, harassed, hounded and put to death outside the walls of his nation's capital city. As your fellow citizens in this *Borough, in our Diocese and County*, we express sorrow for those ways in which we have failed to welcome and to reverence the image of God in *you/them*, and for the way in which we have turned friends into outsiders. We pledge ourselves to walk with all who seek refuge in this and in every community, by sharing now the journey God calls us to walk towards healing and hope.

1. Jesus is condemned to die

As refugees and asylum seekers, sometimes it seems as if there is no place for us to find rest. We are shackled to our fate, surrounded by a world of pain. We wait to take the next frightening journey. We carry with us the torment of our past. Weighed down with all that, we must now find the strength for another walk. But, handcuffed to injustice as we are, we are determined to find the strength for one more journey. We will indeed take the long walk through despair to freedom and hope.

Prayer
Help us, O God, to recognise that we have the inner strength to move from being victims to survivors, and to know that with your help we can even be victors over all the pain we carry in our minds, hearts, and bodies. Amen.

2. Jesus carries his cross

As if the inner burden of past pain is not enough, now as refugees and asylum seekers we must shoulder a new weight of suffering inflicted by people who don't understand this past, this pain. Don't people realise it's such an effort just to get up every morning, to be on the journey through life at all?

Prayer
Help us, O God, to create space for the stories and experiences each of us carries, so that, unburdening ourselves, we will be free to make the contribution you call all of us to make to our common life. Amen.

3. Jesus falls the first time

We stagger beneath the weight of our story, of history. Rejection, pain, suffering: all play their part in our continuing drama. We look backwards. We fall backwards towards the pain of our past. Will the memories lead to our collapse? Or will we find behind us the arms of new friends to support our recovery?

Prayer

Help us, O God, to be your loving arms in the world, to console, to embrace and to support all who have been damaged by the torments of inhuman behaviour. Amen.

4. Jesus meets his mother

We remember home, family, friends. In the confusion of events inside our heads, we see a vision of a loved one from whom we are now separated, exiled by thousands of miles. This person walks towards us to soothe our suffering, to cleanse us and bring us healing.

Prayer

Help us, O God, to be gentle with one another, sensitive to our feelings of loss and exile, for we are far from home. Give us a vision of how we may be healed. Amen.

5. Simon helps carry the cross

A person, perhaps reluctantly at first, stops to help us. For a while we feel that the weight of our story, of the history we carry with us, is now at least shared. Someone cares. Someone will listen. Will this person become our friend?

Prayer

Help us, O God, to shoulder the complexity of each other's histories. Even though we can never know all the ins and outs, make us sensitive to the fact that our stories are holy ground, the ground in which you plant the seeds of your kingdom. Amen.

6. Veronica wipes Jesus' face

It was all confusing, a dream, a terrible and horrific nightmare. It seemed to be about someone else, not us. But we now awake to discover that it's true. We've been dreaming about our story. We are sweating. We are gripped with fear. The pain of our past is all around us. But then we feel the softness of a friendly hand, wiping our brow. 'It will be all right', this person gently assures us.

Prayer
Help us, O God, to wipe away the tears, the guilt, the anxiety with which we live, day by day. Amen.

7. Jesus falls the second time

The memories of what we have endured return. We can never seem to escape the power of the people who made us suffer in the past. Our mind whirls. Somehow, we stagger on, but are we ever going to make it through?

Prayer
Help us, O God, to work through our memories of all that we have suffered, so that though we cannot change the past, we may begin to transform its consequences for us today. Amen.

8. Jesus meets the women of Jerusalem

Some days are easier than others. The pain is always there, but we can at least hide it. We meet friends in the street and put on a brave face. But behind the arm we lift to greet them, our dragging feet show that life is getting us down.

Prayer
Help us, O God, not to bury our pain, but to find those with whom we can share it, so that we can truly greet others with and in the joy of knowing that our burden is being lifted. Amen.

9. Jesus falls the third time

When things are bad for us, they are in fact desperate. It is like being caught in a spiral from which we can never be free. Everything spins around us. O God, make it stop.

Prayer
Help us, O Lord, on our worst days, to know that somewhere you are there for us, because you are not beyond our pain and suffering, you are actually in it. Amen.

10. Jesus is stripped

At times we feel utterly naked because our fate is always in the hands of others. We have no control. We are at their mercy.

Prayer
Help us, O God, to cope with powerlessness, and to know that it is when we are at our weakest that we are in fact at our strongest. Amen.

11. Jesus is nailed to the cross

The process by which our case for asylum or for refuge is examined makes us so open and vulnerable. Sometimes people just don't realise this. They don't know how painful the wounds are.

Prayer
Help us, O God, to recognise just how close to the edge we live our lives, and to know that this is where we find you too. Amen.

12. Jesus dies on the cross

Sometimes it feels as if everyone and everything is against us. We are banging ourselves against a brick wall. In fact we are finished.

Prayer
Help us, O God, even when it feels like death is the only answer, to know that in the despair, in the void, even in the silence, you are there. Amen.

13. Jesus is taken down from the cross

We have nothing left to give. Someone must literally pick us up and show us how the journey through life is going to continue. It's just all too complicated, too much to bear.

Prayer
Help us, O God, to be there for each other when it seems that we are finished, so that we can lend a hand, or shoulder an arm and give each other space for new hope to emerge. Amen.

14. Jesus is laid in the tomb

We are lifeless. We sit staring at a blank wall across a table. We don't, we can't even see the people close to us. We are too turned in on ourselves. We stand at a window and look into the street, but everything seems dead. Is there anything to hope for?

Prayer
Help us to know, O God, that when we have given up hope, such death-like experiences are the gaps which you fill with the love of new possibilities. Amen.

15. The resurrection

A friendly smile, a helping hand, a reassuring hug, a listening ear: one or all of these somehow brings us back to life. The pain of our stories will always be there. We will always carry their scars in our minds, our hearts, our bodies, but these won't continue to dictate our lives. We have survived. We are free. We will be victorious over everything and anything that life can throw at us.

Prayer
Help us, O God, to recognise that we do have the inner strength to move from being victims to survivors, and to know that with your help we can even be victors over all the pain we carry in our minds, hearts, and bodies, now and always. Amen.

Chris Chivers
England

Holy Week Communion

Call to worship

Worship God with all your being:
God transcendent, in this place!
Glancing, shifting, dancing spirit,
Immanent, the source of grace.
> **Face to face with God we honour**
> **values that the Christ would crown,**
> **we would risk divine communion,**
> **see the world turned upside down.**

Andrew Pratt
England

Hymn

First the cheering, then the jeering –
crowds can change their minds at will.
First they hail him, then condemn him;
aim to please, or aim to kill.

First the anger, then the whipping,
clearing out the Temple court.
First the traders, then the money –
space for prayer cannot be bought.

First the perfume, then the poison –
money should not go to waste.
First anointing, then annoyance –
do not judge her deed in haste.

First the trusting, then betrayal –
Judas seeking cash in hand.
First he loved him, then provoked him,
daring him to take a stand.

First the kneeling, then the serving,
showing deep humility.
First bread breaking, then wine sharing –
'Do this as you think of me.'

First the garden, then the praying –
sweating blood, then traitor's kiss.
First the trial, then denial –
Peter, has it come to this?

First the nails and then the hammer
piercing flesh and splitting bone.
First the sighing, then the dying –
Jesus on the cross, alone.

First the grieving, then the praying,
agonising through your death.
First we share your desolation –
while you wait to take new breath.

Tune: Stuttgart

Marjorie Dobson
England

Reading

When it was almost time for the Jewish Passover, Jesus went
up to Jerusalem. In the temple courts he found men selling
cattle, sheep and doves, and others sitting at tables exchanging money. So he made a whip out of cords, and drove all
from the temple area, both sheep and cattle; he scattered the
coins of the money changers and overturned their tables. To
those who sold doves he said, 'Get these out of here! How
dare you turn my Father's house into a market!'

His disciples remembered that it is written: 'Zeal for your
house will consume me.'

Then the Jews demanded of him, 'What miraculous sign
can you show us to prove your authority to do all this?'

Jesus answered them, 'Destroy this temple, and I will raise
it again in three days.'

The Jews replied, 'It has taken forty-six years to build this
temple, and you are going to raise it in three days?' But the
temple he had spoken of was his body. After he was raised
from the dead, his disciples recalled what he had said. Then
they believed the Scripture and the words that Jesus had
spoken.

(John 2.13–22 New International Version)

Hymn

Love inspired the anger
That cleared a temple court,
Overturned the wisdom
Which their greed had wrought.

Love inspired the anger
That set the leper free
From the legal strictures
That brought misery.

Love inspired the anger
That cursed a viper's brood:
Set on domination,
Self with God confused.

Love inspires the anger
That curses poverty,
Preaches life's enrichment,
Seeks equality.

Love inspires the anger
That still can set us free
From the world's conventions
Bringing liberty.

Tune: North Coates

Andrew Pratt
England

The Peace

There was anger.
There still is.
But we come in peace.
Let us offer a sign of that peace to each other.

Hymn

(Based on an interpretation of the Lord's Prayer attributed to Jim Cotter)

Earth-maker, source of the world and our wisdom,
lover and carer, forever the same.
Bread for our sustenance, all we have needed,
you offer freely, we worship your name.

Pain-bearer, holding the fragile and faulted,
loving the broken and tending the frail;
bringing forgiveness and grace for our mending,
you are the heaven where love will not fail.

Life-giver, offering justice and mercy,
needing your presence we come at your call;
hallow your name though the whole of creation,
you reign in glory for ever and all!

Tune: Stewardship

Andrew Pratt
England

The Lord's Supper – Thanksgiving

Narrator: Thirteen men met round the table that evening,
ready to celebrate the memory of one great his-
torical break for freedom. They were excited and
full of the events of the week in the city, laughing
and talking and exchanging stories.

Only two of them knew that the night would
end with a betrayal that would lead to tragedy.

What a collection of men they were! Several
tough, argumentative, forthright, north country
fishermen, a tax collector, a fervent Jewish
nationalist, a couple who were concerned with
money – one about overspending, one about

acquiring more – another who was never very sure of himself, or of anyone else, and several who kept their heads down and seemed to be content to be background figures.

The conversation and the wine flowed freely and for most of the men it seemed like any other Passover feast. Occasionally someone asked Jesus a question and the room quietened while he answered. One or two of them had private words with him, but that was not unusual, some had always been in a kind of inner circle.

But no one took much notice of the fact that Judas was acting even more strangely than ever, jumpy and nervous and very aware of the time they were taking with the meal. He had always kept himself slightly apart from the others and was sometimes critical of the way Jesus behaved, so he was not the most popular member of the group. Perhaps that is why no one could really remember when he left the room. The rest of them carried on talking and waited to see what Jesus wanted to do next.

When the supper was finished, there was a break in the conversation.

In the sudden silence, Jesus picked up bread and broke it in pieces.

Jesus: This bread is my body and I am broken for you and others like you. Take a piece, each of you, and eat it.

Narrator: As they did that, he lifted the cup of wine.

Jesus: Blood

Narrator: he said

Jesus: my blood. I'll be spilling it for you and for everyone else. Drink, please, all of you.

Narrator: They didn't understand the significance of what he said, but they did as he asked.

Jesus: You'll never forget this night,

Narrator: he said.

Jesus: Each time you break bread and drink wine, you'll remember me.

Narrator: He was right. They did remember – and, even today, so do we, as we break bread and drink wine together.

Marjorie Dobson
England

The Breaking of the Bread

When we break bread we share in the body of Christ.
For though we are many, we are one.

The Sharing of the Bread and Wine

Hymn

The story stands, a memory remains:
that night of crisis, time of chance and choice;
prefigurement of death, eternal gains,
a time to meet with fear, or to rejoice.

That tangled gang of misbegotten men
had gathered with their master for a meal.
Though Passover they celebrate again,
his words were enigmatic, stark, yet real.

262

The wine was wine, the bread was only bread.
What was that talk of body and of blood?
They strained to understand the things he said,
make sense of every symbol as they should.

Yet, if the meal we share is more than act,
a play with words, mere taste of bread and wine,
then we must demonstrate the living fact
that love is always part of God's design.

Tune: Woodlands

Andrew Pratt
England

Prayers

We have not forgotten that night, Lord.
Together we have remembered it and remembered your
sacrifice.

Those men were changed by their experience
and we are too.

Help us to demonstrate the living fact
that sacrificial love is always part of your design.

Marjorie Dobson
England

Extempore intercessory prayers may be offered at this point.

Hymn

Jesus the carpenter, hanging on Calvary,
nails through your feet and your work-hardened hands –
wood you have worked with and wood is your destiny –
paying the price of our sinful demands.

You came to our world as a part of a family,
living and learning the carpenter's trade.
You followed your father's instructions so faithfully,
shaping and crafting the yokes that you made:
Jesus the carpenter ...

You called other workmen to join in your ministry,
laying rough hands on the sick and the lame.
You taught of God's love with such power and authority,
people who knew you believed you insane:
Jesus the carpenter ...

You faced with great courage the open hostility
coming from those who believed they were right.
They stripped you and beat you and laughed at you finally,
thinking your death was the end of the fight:
Jesus the carpenter ...

But we, who now know that you ended triumphantly
working with wood 'til your task was complete,
can come to your cross with our hope and humility,
laying our pride at the carpenter's feet:

Jesus the carpenter, hanging on Calvary,
nails through your feet and your work-hardened hands –
wood you have worked with and wood is your destiny –
paying the price of our sinful demands

Tune: Blow the Wind Southerly

Marjorie Dobson
England

Blessing

From a stall in a stable to a cross on a hill, wood was your way of life, Christ the carpenter. Bless us now in our lives that whatever our destiny we will walk the way to it with the same courage and determination as you had.
Amen.

Marjorie Dobson
England

In the Light of the Morning

In the light of this morning, we come to God in worship.
In the light of Christ, we seek to see ourselves as he sees us.
In the light of his living Spirit, we look at the world he
    loves.

And so, we offer our worship and thanksgiving in this Easter season. We rejoice in the love that can overcome death and live again, showing itself through the love of others. Sometimes we are surprised to find that love where we least expect it.

In this morning's light, Lord, open our eyes, our minds and our hearts to the truth you have to reveal to us. Help us to see that you live and love even where we find it hard to see you. Give us a wider vision and make us ready to respond to every expression of your love.

Let us know your living presence in our worship
and be encouraged to live your love in the world.

Amen.

Wendy Ross-Barker
England

At the Tomb

(A Prayer Litany for Easter Morning)

Voice One: Woman, why are you weeping?

First Woman: We mourn these dark days of death and
 denial.
Abandoned, betrayed, forsaken.
Left alone. Jesus gone.
Where have they laid him?

Voice One: Woman, why are you weeping?

Second Woman: We are afraid for our Lord.
Humiliated in both life and death.
Robbed from the grave.
O where have they laid him?

Voice Two: Mary, do not hold on to me.

Voice One: Women, why are you weeping?

Women: We weep for Jesus, missing.
We weep for Columbian kin, missing.
We weep for children entangled in bitter
 domestic disputes, missing.

Voice One: Men, why are you weeping?

Men: We weep for Jesus, humiliated and
 tortured.
We weep for all political prisoners,
 suffering at the hands of oppressors.
We weep for Muslims vilified by world
 powers and the media.
We weep for peaceful protestors
 violently opposed.

266

Voice One: Women, why are you weeping?

Women: We weep for Jesus, abandoned and alone.
We weep for the elderly, separated from
family and community.
We weep for children, orphaned by AIDS.
We weep for the young, devastated by
war.

Voice Two: Do not hold on to me as I was.
For I am with you, now, in the least of
these.
As you weep for them, you weep for me.
As you serve them, you serve me.

All: Alleluia! Christ is risen!
Christ lives in the gardener,
in the immigrant who mows our lawns
and trims our shrubs.
Christ lives in the teacher,
the day care worker who minds our
children.
Christ lives in the tortured,
the prisoners of 'the war on terrorism'.
Christ lives in those for whom we weep.

Alleluia!
Christ is risen!
Christ is risen indeed!

Ana K. Gobledale
USA/Australia

Reflection on Resurrection Hope

Come Look, Go Tell

As a member of the Christian community I believe that Christ has risen and Christ is alive today.

My understanding of resurrection is that God's love has always been with us and remains unchanged. Jesus did not have to die to turn God into a gracious and loving God. Rather, Jesus revealed to us the out-reaching, all-inclusive, persuasive compassion of God.

This understanding would say that Easter continues to happen whenever and wherever people find themselves able to start again. Wherever there is reconciliation and healing, wherever there is life and wholeness, there is resurrection.

Easter is the untiring hope of light and life, however deep our present darkness and suffering. In the midst of grief, loss and sorrow, hope is re-born, and we can start again. It's never too late to make a new start, because God is with us and known to us above all through the life, ministry and death of Jesus of Nazareth.

The Easter experiences happen again and again as the story is re-told in history and through generations and is handed on from parents to children, from one culture to another. Christ died on the cross and rose again. Christ is alive!

What is this Easter experience?

It is that of walking through the valley of death and discovering that Christ is alive, who leads us out into new life, hope and joy. It is living in hard and difficult situations and discovering that Christ is alive and walking with us, leading us into the dawn of a new day.

These hard and difficult situations come in many forms. For some it is when everything that seemed sharp and clear suddenly becomes unfocused; the picture breaks up, and we have to start all over again. For others it is a sickness of body, mind or spirit and for others it is the loss of a friend, a companion, a loved one.

I would almost go as far as to suggest that unless we experience the valley of the shadow of death and difficult situations, the Easter resurrection may remain just a story two thousand years old. But when we walk the valley of the shadow of death we discover that Christ is there, walking with us, leading us into a dawn of the new day. Then we can know that Christ is alive.

We experience the resurrection individually but I believe that Resurrection is primarily about community.

Mary Magdalen discovers the empty tomb and immediately shares the not-yet-understood experience with Simon Peter and the disciples. Some of the disciples fail to grasp what has happened and some believe. Mary stays by the tomb, encounters the risen Christ and immediately returns to share the message.

Our own individual resurrection experience is only one part of a community of resurrection experiences; experiences that encourage the community of faith to foster and maintain the essence of resurrection life, and proclaim resurrection week by week in story and in the breaking of bread. It is a community in which we share each other's stories of resurrection so that, learning from others we can enter more deeply into the experience of our own and each other's new life.

Resurrection is an experience to be shared in church and society recognizing that as individuals we have many different shadow of death experiences; we know pain and suffering in many different ways.

In society, it is known in poverty, homelessness, violence, child abuse, racism, and environmental destruction of our world. But when there is death, there is always the possibility of resurrection.

As Christians we are called to share our resurrection experiences so that our society and world may also know that Christ is alive. The church is called to struggle and work in partnership with the world in the work and mission of Christ, enabling new life to spring from the valley and the tomb.

The Risen Christ said to Mary: 'Do not hold on to me.'

We are called to free the risen Christ from the bondage of the institutional church. Together we will discover that even out of the darkest and most seemingly hopeless situations, the hope of new life is possible.

If Christ is alive within us today, then let us go and share this hope in the community, share it with each other and share it in the world. Wherever in the world there is violence or suffering of any kind, let us be there. We will continue to learn from the man Jesus, from the one who later became known as the Risen Christ, tell the Good News, show the Good News, be the Good News.

Saikolone Taufa
Aotearoa New Zealand

Old Blue Shirt

This morning I peg the clothes
your old, blue work shirt.

So many times I have
mended and washed this faded cloth.

But today it seems
that you are alive again
when I watch your old blue shirt
dancing with the wind.

Denise Bennett
England

Travelling

Why is the journey out
so much longer than
the journey back?
Are there more miles?
Or is it simply
a matter of perspective?

Can the way we travel forward,
not knowing what lies ahead,
make the distance
stretch beyond existing length
into an eternity
of longing to be there,
with the journey safely ended?

And, as we turn
from what we have attained
back to the known
and pre-existing,
is it the familiarity
of signposts passed before
that makes the returning
so much swifter?

Or is there something deeper,
more profound;
that travelling once
a new uncharted way
makes viewpoints change,
so that this road,
this journey,
can never be the same again?

Marjorie Dobson
England

A Ruined Abbey

This abbey used to fret small hours
of belief like clothes moths in winter.
Monks syncopated praise
in young days at Lauds.

Pheasants' eyes embered in red,
flinched as bells authorised Prime,
Brothers quenched their conceits
in prayer and whispered to the Son.

Each winter, old men axed
iced ditches and watched
black canons, heads huddled,
cross the barbican for Terce.

In the gatehouse at Sext, the abbot
glanced to the village where
frost signed his fields and empty
trees still showed the light.

Snow shaded a badgers' sett
as a cadence of psalms
at None tracked last things:
the dying, impatient for ecstasy.

Before Vespers, early stars awaited
Orion; a procession of nomad
swans settled on black water;
monks were attentive, expectant.

Now, even with its veins opened,
the abbey stays a place for hope
and lures us back for Compline.
Grant us a quiet night and a perfect end.

Derek Webster
England

Gnarled Old Trees

Gnarled old trees
lie broken
and dead,
struck down in their prime,
no longer bearing fruit
or growing
through the cycle of the seasons.

Yet in their brokenness
is beauty,
timeless
weathered out beauty.

It was their time to die,
for in their dying
they sustain the life of others.

A honeycomb grows
deep inside the hollow,
bringing sweetness to the death.

Butterflies dance
around the textured bark.

Lichens and mosses
root in the crevices;
new life
where once the sap did flow.

Heavenly dragonflies
hover.

Beauty from brokenness ...
life from death ...

Pat Marsh
England

Index of Authors

Index of Titles

5 Hope for Today's World

6 Worshipping the God of Hope

7 Christ Our Eternal Hope

Acknowledgements and Sources

1 The Nature of Hope

Advent is a Time of Hope, Andrew Pratt © Stainer and Bell Ltd
Advent Peace Prayers © Carol Penner

Cause for Joy © John Johansen-Berg
Celtic Pilgrimage, A © Carole Ellefsen-Jones
Come Sing a Song of Faith, Marjorie Dobson © Stainer and Bell
Cries of Advent © Janet Lees from *Edged with Fire*, United Reformed
    Church Prayer Handbook 1994

Deep Healing © Janet Lees
Door, The © John Johansen-Berg

Epiphany Peace Prayer, A © Carol Penner

Faith Offers the Promise of Hope © Wendy Whitehead

God's Hands © Claire Smith
Gossamer Trust © Pat Marsh from *Silent Strength* published by
    Inspire 2005

Hope, Mary Brogan from *Journey to the Millennium* © National Board
    of Catholic Women

I Believe that God Can and Will Let Good Arise © Dietrich
    Bonhoeffer ©Translation David Bunney
I Turn to You © Melanie Frew
I Wait © Richard Becher
Infant, The © Eve Jackson
It's Advent-time © Kim Fabricius

Journeying in Hope © Jan Berry from *Gateways of Grace*, United Reformed Church Prayer Handbook 1998/1999

Live with Faith © Colin Ferguson
Living Lord of Justice Providing Hope © Geoffrey Duncan
Lord of the Evening © Pat Marsh from *Silent Strength* published by Inspire 2005
Lord of the Journey © Peter Graystone

Mirror of Glory © Wendy d Ward
Movement, The © Claire Smith

New Life for Old © Heather Pencavel
Nomalanga's Story © Tod Gobledale

O Come, O Come Emmanuel © Carol Penner
On Seeing 'A Daisy' in a Frame © Eve Jackson

Prayer for All Who are Addicted, A © Carol Penner
Prayer for All Who Live with Violence, A © Carol Penner
Prayer for Healing, A © Carol Penner
Prayer to the Prince of Peace, A © Carol Penner

Rainbow Promise © Elizabeth Gray-King
Reflection © Catholic Women's Weekly
Return, The © Claire Smith

Sacrifice © Elizabeth Smith
Sight © Claire Smith
Speaking of Hope ... © Eve Jackson
Sunrise – Sunset, Marjorie Dobson © Stainer and Bell

Tenacity © Abigail Joy Tobler
Thomas © Brian Louis Pearce
Transform the World © Edmund Shehadeh
Travelling to Bethlehem © Janet Lees from *Edged with Fire*, United Reformed Church Prayer Handbook 1994

Waiting © Janet Lees and Bob Warwicker from *Edged with Fire*, United Reformed Church Prayer Handbook 1994
We Believe in God © Joerg Zink and Rainer Roehricht © Translation David Bunney
When You Hope © Margaret Louise Granahan
Word, The © Claire Smith

2 When Life Seems Hopeless

Children Die from Drought and Earthquake © Kim Fabricius
Communion Hymn in Time of Moral Famine, A © Edward Moran

Demanding God © Alma Fritchley
Desert © Cecily Taylor
Doing the Impossible, St Francis of Assisi

Eye for an Eye, An © Mahatma Gandhi

Face to Face © Wendy Whitehead
For Survivors of Abuse © Carol Penner
From Dependency to Self-Reliance © Anil K. Patil

God of Understanding © Alma Fritchley
Grief in Iraq © John Stephenson

Hope Comes in the Morning © Jan Berry from *Gateways of Grace*,
    United Reformed Church Prayer Handbook 1998/1999

Hope for All God's People © Kelvin Harris
Hopeless or Hopeful? © Eleanore Milardo
Hopelessness © John Johansen-Berg
Hope is Always There, Marjorie Dobson © Stainer and Bell
Hospital Corners © Roger Grainger
How I Wish © Janet Lees
Humane © Wendy d Ward
Humanism © Wendy d Ward

I Asked © Eve Jackson
I Don't Really Comprehend, Andrew Pratt © Stainer and Bell

Just Call Me Martha © Melanie Frew

Letter to Dominic and Gregory © Chris Chivers
Lichen © Abigail Joy Tobler
Lost Hope © Elizabeth Gray-King

Mary with John © Brian Louis Pearce
May the Light of Justice Shine © Jan Berry from *Gateways of Grace*,
    United Reformed Church Prayer Handbook 1998/1999

Not So This Christmas © Wendy Ross-Barker

Pandora's Lament © Rose James
Poverty © Harry Wiggett
Prayer Against Violence © Carol Penner
Prayer for Male Survivors of Violence © Carol Penner
Prayer in Response to the Rwandan Genocide © Chris Chivers
Prisoners of Hope! © Graham Adams

Reflections upon Ramallah in Poetic Form – My Key Your Key ©
  Glenn Jetta Barclay
Refugee, Refugee Grow in Hope © Glenn Jetta Barclay
Remove the Roadblocks © Geoffrey Duncan
Runaways © Bob Warwicker from *Edged with Fire*, United Reformed
  Church Prayer Handbook 1994

Silent Cry, The © Harry Wiggett
Six Angles on Depression © Janet Lees
Song of Resistance © Graham Adams
Sudanese Refugee Helps Others © John Ball

Unwed Mother © Harry Wiggett

View from the Edge, A © Jessica Hope Isherwood

When Hope Is … © Janet Lees
When the World Appears to be Against Us © Duncan Tuck
Where are the Mathematics of God? © Glenn Jetta Barclay
Where is God? © Graham Adams

3 Spirit of Hope

Be Kind to Yourself © Anil K. Patil
Blessing for Parents © Carol Penner
Body Prayer, A © Carol Penner

Circles of Hope © Eleanore Milardo

For Moira © Elizabeth Gray-King
For Those Who Make the Arpilleras © Fiona Ritchie Walker
Fundacion Solidaridad – Teresa's Story © Fiona Ritchie Walker

Gift of Hope, The © Raymond Chapman from *Stations of the Nativity* published by The Canterbury Press
Good News! © Wendy Whitehead

Hope © Jessica Hope Isherwood
Hope, the Phoenix © Christine Ractliff

I Am Greater than My Thinking © W. L. Wallace
I Am Strong © Eleanore Milardo
I Am the Living Vine © Norm S. D. Esdon
I Met You in the Most Unexpected Place © Melanie Frew
In My Silence, Anonymous
Into the Unknown © Jan Berry from *Gateways of Grace*, United Reformed Church Prayer Handbook 1998/1999
Island of Hope © John Roberts
I Will Give You Hope © Melanie Frew

Journey of Self-Acceptance, A © Sarah Ingle

Laughter in Her Eyes © Jill Jenkins

Miriama © Glenn Jetta Barclay

O God Whose Nature and Name is LOVE © Jean Mortimer
Our God Shall Be a Shelter © Edward Moran

Prayer for Playing, A © Carol Penner
Prayer of Remembering and Confession © Tod and Ana Gobledale

Robin © Eve Jackson

Sing for Harmony © John Johansen-Berg
Sometimes a Word Surprises © Glenn Jetta Barclay
Strange Tongues © Marjorie Dobson

Those Who Can't Speak Will Shout © Maureen R. Davis
Thought ... © Cate Adams
Trade Union Prayer © Cate Adams

Where There is Good News © John Johansen-Berg
Words of Waiting © Wendy Ross-Barker

4 Springs of Hope

Advent Affirmations © Graham Adams
Advent Hope © Annabel Shilson-Thomas/CAFOD

Beatitudes for Those Who Work with Disabled People, Author
    Unknown
Beatitudes – Upside-Down World © Bernard Thorogood
Beatitudes: We Remember, The © Annabel Shilson-Thomas
Blessèd are You © Melanie Frew

Coming for Many © Duncan L. Tuck from *Courage to Love* compiled
    by Geoffrey Duncan and published by Darton, Longman and Todd

Feeding 5,000 or More © Graham Adams
Fruit of the Spirit © John Johansen-Berg

Gentle Spirit, Now Embracing © Michael Jacob Kooiman
God of Love and Love Abundant © David J. Harding
Great Joy! © Geoffrey Duncan

Here Is the News, Cecily Taylor © Stainer and Bell
How Can We Stand, Ignoring Each Injustice?, Andrew Pratt © Stainer
    and Bell
Hope for the World: Baptism in a Multi-racial Family of Faith © Carla
    A. Grosch-Miller

I Am the Bread of Life © Norm S. D. Esdon
I Am the Light of the World © Norm S. D. Esdon

Morning Prayer © Carol Penner
My Creed – My Beatitude © Geoffrey Duncan from *Courage to Love*
    compiled by Geoffrey Duncan and published by Darton Longman
    and Todd

Paraphrase of the Beatitudes, A © W. L. Wallace
Reach Out to Our Humanity © Annabel Shilson-Thomas/CAFOD
Roots, Shoots and Fruits © Nick Butler

Seeing Christ's Face in Haiti © Ana K. Gobledale

Waiting with Hope © Geoffrey Duncan

5 Hope for Today's World

Africa © Melanie Flew
After Ascension © Wendy Ross-Barker
All Creation Hopes © Pearl Willemssen Hoffman

be-*Christ*-ing Church © Graham Adams

Celebrating Christmas © Astrid Lobo Gajiwala
Celebration of Hope © John Johansen-Berg
Commitment to Hope © Louise Margaret Granahan

Dreamer at Prayer © Wendy Whitehead
Dough is Rising,The © W. L. Wallace

Flower, The © Ed Cox from *Justice Joy and Jubilee*, United Reformed
   Church Prayer Handbook 1999/2000
From the Deep Recesses of Our Souls, We Cry Out ... © Sharon Rose
   Joy Ruis-Duremdes. Used with Permission.
Future Tense and Present Tense © Bernard Thorogood

God Comes in Unexpected Ways, Andrew Pratt © Stainer and Bell
   Ltd
God Is Known in Many Ways © Wendy Ross-Barker
God Who Creates and then Colours the Earth © Kim Fabricius

Hope in the Lord © Heather Johnston
Hope Where Are You? © Jean Brookes
Hoping and Longing for Change and Release © Wendy Ross-Barker
Hoping In God's Dream © David Tutty
Hymn upon the Publication of a Church Cookbook © Edward Moran

I Am A Loveable, Creative Person © W. L. Wallace from *Courage to
   Love* compiled by Geoffrey Duncan and published by Darton,
   Longman and Todd
I Am the Doorway © Norm S. D. Esdon
I Am the Way © Norm S. D. Esdon
I Dream of a Church © Kate Compston
In Celebration of Unconventional Friendships © Jean Mortimer
In Our Silence © Eve Jackson

Just One Year © Tod and Ana Gobledale

6 Worshipping the God of Hope

Amid the Many Thoughts © W. L. Wallace
As We Meet to Offer Worship, Andrew Pratt © Stainer and Bell

Benediction for Hope © Louise Margaret Granahan

Candles © Colin Ferguson
Christmas Bliss © Wendy d Ward
City Where All Share the Feast, A © David Fox
Closing Blessing © Jan Berry
Come By Here © Wendy Ross-Barker
Creative Creator © Geoffrey Duncan

Dance, The © Eleanore Milardo

Easter Blessing © Graham Adams
Easter Vitality © Peter Graystone
Enthusiastic Hope that Broadens Expectation © Andrew Pratt
Evening Prayer © Carol Penner

Feed Nations with Your Love © Eve Jackson
First Remembered Christmas © Denise Bennett

Go from Here Full of Hope © Peter Graystone
God Be with You © Marjorie Dobson
God Give us Hope © Jan Berry
God of Creativity © Geoffrey Duncan
Green Woodpecker © Denise Bennett

Harvest © Annabel Shilson-Thomas/CAFOD
Hope © Sarah Ingle
Hope has a Heartbeat © Carla A. Grosch-Miller
Holy Spirit, Sudden Gust © Kim Fabricius
How Can the Time of Peace Come to Earth? © W. L. Wallace

I Saw the Gardener Dancing © W. L. Wallace
Inspirational God © Marjorie Dobson

Joys to Come © Denise Bennett

Let us Worship Together © Elizabeth Joy
Life-giving God © Chris Esdaile and Alison Facey

Litany of Hope in Solidarity © Annabel Shilson-Thomas/CAFOD

Multi-faith Food Blessing © W. L. Wallace

New Hopefulness, A © Graham Adams
Nothing is Impossible with God © Jill Jenkins

Our Living and Challenging God © Janet Wootton

Radiance © Wendy d Ward

Shining with Hope © Peter Graystone
Stainbeck © Jean Mortimer

Tender God © United Society for the Propagation of the Gospel.
    Permission Sought

Walk with Us © Geoffrey Duncan

7 Christ Our Eternal Hope

At the Tomb © Ana K. Gobledale

Beginning © Derek Webster
Blessing – from a Stall in a Stable © Marjorie Dobson

Crocus © Hannah Warwicker

Earth-maker Source of the World, © Andrew Pratt
Easter © Wendy Ross-Barker
Easter Hope © Annabel Shilson-Thomas/CAFOD
Easter Litany © Annabel Shilson-Thomas/CAFOD

First the Cheering then the Jeering, Marjorie Dobson © Stainer and
    Bell Ltd
Food that Lasts © Janet Lees from *Edged with Fire*, United Reformed
    Church Prayer Handbook 1994

God Marks No Ending, Only New Beginnings © Andrew Pratt
Gnarled Old Trees © Pat Marsh from *Silent Strength* published by
    Inspire 2005

Holy Week Communion © Andrew Pratt and Marjorie Dobson
Hope Against Hope © Brian Louis Pearce
Hope of Resurrection © David Fox

I Am the Resurrection and the Life © Norm S. D. Esdon
In the Light of the Morning © Wendy Ross-Barker

Jesus is Risen © Kim Fabricius
Jesus the Carpenter Hanging on Calvary, Marjorie Dobson © Stainer
    and Bell Ltd
Journey with Jesus the Refugee, The © Chris Chivers

Life © Claire Smith
Living and Dying © Heather Pencavel
Lord's Supper – Thanksgiving, The © Marjorie Dobson
Loss of Hope © Raymond Chapman from *A Pastoral Prayer Book*
    published by The Canterbury Press
Love Inspired the Anger © Andrew Pratt

Mountains of Pain © Claire Smith

Not Yet! © Stephen Brown from *Gateways of Grace*, United Reformed
    Church Prayer Handbook 1998/1999
Now That I'm Gone © Fiona Ritchie Walker

Old Blue Shirt © Denise Bennett
On the Beach: Easter Sunrise © Derek Webster
Our Hope of Freedom Beyond Death © Heather Johnston

Planting my Father © Denise Bennett
Prayer of Confession © Nick Butler
Promised Thing, The © Elizabeth Gray-King

Quaker Burial Ground © Denise Bennett

Reflection on Resurrection Hope © Saikolone Taufa
Remembering © Fiona Ritchie Walker
Resurrection NOW! © Janet Lees from *Edged with Fire*, United
    Reformed Church Prayer Handbook 1994
Risen Lord © Annabel Shilson-Thomas/CAFOD
Ruined Abbey, A © Derek Webster

Story Stands, a Memory Remains, The, Andrew Pratt © Stainer and
    Bell Ltd